JEREMIAH J. JOHNSTON

UNANSWERED

LASTING TRUTH FOR TRENDING QUESTIONS

LifeWay Press®; Nashville, Tennessee

Published by LifeWay Press® • © 2015 Christian Thinkers Corporation

ISBN 978-1-4300-3959-4 • Item 005717983

Dewey decimal classification: 230
Subject headings: LIFE \ CHRISTIANITY \ BIBLE—STUDY

To order additional copies of this resource, write to LifeWay Resources Customer Service; One LifeWay Plaza; Nashville, TN 37234-0113; order online at www.lifeway.com; fax 615.251.5933; phone toll free 800.458.2772; email orderentry@lifeway.com; or visit the LifeWay Christian Store serving you.

Printed in the United States of America

Groups Ministry Publishing • LifeWay Resources
One LifeWay Plaza • Nashville, TN 37234-0152

CONTENTS

ABOUT THE AUTHOR

Dr. Jeremiah J. Johnston is a New Testament scholar, professor, pastor, apologist, and regular speaker on university campuses, at churches, and at conferences. His passion is equipping Christians to give intellectually informed accounts of what they believe. Jeremiah completed his doctoral residency in Oxford in partnership with the Oxford Centre for Mission Studies and received his PhD from Middlesex University (United Kingdom), with commendation. He has master's degrees from Acadia University (Canada) and Midwestern Baptist Theological Seminary (United States). He has lectured throughout the United States, Canada, and the United Kingdom.

Jeremiah serves as the founder and president of Christian Thinkers Society, a Resident Institute at Houston Baptist University, where he also serves as Associate Professor of early Christianity. Christian Thinkers Society produces live events, media productions, conferences, and publications to teach pastors and Christians to become thinkers and thinkers to become Christians. Jeremiah resides in Houston, Texas, with his wife and two children. For more information visit *www.christianthinkers.com*.

In addition to his popular publications, Jeremiah has distinguished himself with publications in scholarly, refereed journals and serials. These include entries in Oxford University Press and E. J. Brill reference works. He specializes in Christian origins; Jesus and the Gospels; and topics, especially apologetics, that closely relate to Jesus and the Gospels. These include the resurrection of Jesus, New Testament manuscripts (their number, nature, and reliability), extracanonical gospels, resurrection, and afterlife beliefs. He has presented academic papers at learned meetings and has examined ancient texts (papyri, codices, and the like) at renowned libraries, such as the Griffith Papyrology Room of Oxford University's Bodleian Library and the Beinecke Rare Book and Manuscript Library of Yale University.

FOLLOW JEREMIAH:

@JeremyJohnstonJ
/ChristianThinkersSociety
@Jeremy_J_Johnston
ChristianThinkers.com

HOW TO USE THIS STUDY

Hi, I am Jeremiah, and I am honored to lead you through this Bible study. I live at the intersection of the scholarly and popular worlds; therefore, I have a passion for teaching and inspiring people like you to own your faith and to engage confidently with the world around you. I am honored you have committed to invest your time with me in this study.

This Bible study provides a guided process for individuals and small groups to explore Scriptures that equip believers to offer biblical responses to the following challenging questions:

What do we do when God seems silent?

Why can we trust in the bodily resurrection of Jesus?

How should Christians respond to spiritual darkness and paranormal activity?

How can I know for sure the Bible is true and trustworthy?

What should Christians understand about suicide and mental health?

Why do we experience suffering and pain?

One week of Bible study is devoted to each of these topics, and each week is divided into five days of personal study. In the personal study you will find biblical teaching and interactive questions that will help you understand and apply the teaching.

In addition to the personal study, six group sessions are provided that are designed to spark gospel conversations around brief video teachings. Each group session is divided into three sections:

START focuses participants on the topic of the session's video teaching.
WATCH provides key ideas presented in the video.
RESPOND guides the group in a discussion of the video teaching.

To go deeper in your study, you may want to purchase the book *Unanswered: Lasting Truth for Trending Questions* (Whitaker House, ISBN 978-1-6291-1656-3).

TIPS FOR LEADING A GROUP

PRAYERFULLY PREPARE

Prepare for each meeting by—

REVIEWING the weekly material and group questions ahead of time;
PRAYING for each person in the group.

Ask the Holy Spirit to work through you and the group discussion as you point to Jesus each week through God's Word.

MINIMIZE DISTRACTIONS

Create a comfortable environment. If group members are uncomfortable, they'll be distracted and therefore not engaged in the group experience. Plan ahead by taking into consideration—

SEATING, TEMPERATURE, LIGHTING, FOOD OR DRINK, SURROUNDING NOISE, AND GENERAL CLEANLINESS.

At best, thoughtfulness and hospitality show guests and group members they're welcome and valued in whatever environment you choose to gather. At worst, people may never notice your effort, but they're also not distracted. Do every-thing in your ability to help people focus on what's most important: connecting with God, with the Bible, and with one another.

INCLUDE OTHERS

Your goal is to foster a community in which people are welcome just as they are but encouraged to grow spiritually. Always be aware of opportunities to—

INCLUDE any people who visit the group;
INVITE new people to join your group.

ENCOURAGE DISCUSSION

A good small-group experience has the following characteristics.

EVERYONE PARTICIPATES. Encourage everyone to ask questions, share responses, or read aloud.

NO ONE DOMINATES—NOT EVEN THE LEADER. Be sure that your time speaking as a leader takes up less than half of your time together as a group. Politely guide discussion if anyone dominates.

NOBODY IS RUSHED THROUGH QUESTIONS. Don't feel that a moment of silence is a bad thing. People often need time to think about their responses to questions they've just heard or to gain courage to share what God is stirring in their hearts.

INPUT IS AFFIRMED AND FOLLOWED UP. Make sure you point out something true or helpful in a response. Don't just move on. Build community with follow-up questions, asking how other people have experienced similar things or how a truth has shaped their understanding of God and the Scripture you're studying. People are less likely to speak up if they fear that you don't actually want to hear their answers or that you're looking for only a certain answer.

GOD AND HIS WORD ARE CENTRAL. Opinions and experiences can be helpful, but God has given us the truth. Trust Scripture to be the authority and God's Spirit to work in people's lives. You can't change anyone, but God can. Continually point people to the Word and to active steps of faith.

KEEP CONNECTING

Think of ways to connect with group members during the week. Participation during the group session is always improved when members spend time connecting with one another outside the group sessions. The more people are comfortable with and involved in one another's lives, the more they'll look forward to being together. When people move beyond being friendly to truly being friends who form a community, they come to each session eager to engage instead of merely attending. Encourage group members with thoughts, commitments, or questions from the session by connecting through—

EMAILS, TEXTS, AND SOCIAL MEDIA.

When possible, build deeper friendships by planning or spontaneously inviting group members to join you outside your regularly scheduled group time for—

**MEALS; FUN ACTIVITIES; AND
PROJECTS AROUND YOUR HOME, CHURCH, OR COMMUNITY.**

GOD ON MUTE

WHAT DO WE DO WHEN GOD SEEMS SILENT?

START

Welcome to session 1 of *Unanswered*. Tough questions are being asked about Christianity, both inside and outside the church. If we are honest, we as believers sometimes struggle to understand the salient issues of our faith and explain them to our friends who want answers to difficult questions.

We will start by talking about our comfort levels and abilities to respond to tough questions. To get the most out of this study, let's commit to be transparent as we discuss these unanswered questions together.

How comfortable do you usually feel when someone asks you questions about your faith?

How comfortable do you usually feel discussing your own faith questions?

How comfortable did you feel answering the first two questions?

Our purpose in this six-session study is to be equipped, as thoughtful ambassadors of Jesus, to respond to tough questions in a way that attracts people to the truth of Jesus Christ and the Word of God.

Too many Christians are in retreat mode, shying away from the tough questions. This study provides precisely what many people in the church need today: tools and answers. Believers who possess the power to explain and answer tough questions about their faith meet the needs of friends who are searching for the truth. Just as important, they prove that they understand the meaning of their own faith.

Our goal as a group is to leave this study enriched by the truth of Scripture, characterized by a thinking faith, equipped to communicate confidently, and committed to escape the tendency to offer trite answers to a skeptical world.

In session 1 we will begin by seeking the answer to the tough question, What do we do when God seems silent?

WATCH

1. God's silence is real, biblical, personal, common, and not always bad.

2. When the silence is real, I should saturate myself in the psalms.

3. Silence should always lead me to stones of remembrance.

4. The silence of God can lead us from transformation to triumph.

RESPOND

What one truth from Jeremiah's teaching resonated most with you?

Did Jeremiah's discussion of God's silence remind you of a time in your life when God was silent about a particular issue? If you feel comfortable, describe this experience.

In Scripture God called people by name. God never says, "Hey, you!" God is personal and present. Nonetheless, God can sometimes be silent. Two people who experienced both the personal presence and the silence of God were Abram and Sarah. Actually, they experienced the silence of God not once but twice.

Read Genesis 15:1-6.

How would you describe Abram's state of mind and the condition of his heart in this passage?

Try to imagine that. God had promised Abram that through his descendants all the families of the earth would be blessed (see Gen. 12:3), and yet he and his barren wife waited, sometimes not very patiently, to see God's promise become reality. Nothing had worked. The first period of God's silence was 10 years (see Gen. 12–16); the second period of silence, 13 more years (see Gen. 17–18). Abram and Sarah spent nearly 25 years of their lives grappling with God's silence.

What words would you use to describe the relationship the Lord was seeking with Abram?

Abram had been looking around for answers to his uncertainties, but God wanted him to look up. God gave Abram a vision for what He would do through his example of trust and obedience (see Gen. 15:1-6).

If you had been Abram, what would have been going through your mind?

While it might not be the issue of infertility, we can all point to a time in our lives when we have wondered whether God has forgotten us. Imagine that you were in Abram or Sarai's place. For many years God had been silent about how and when His covenant with you would be fulfilled. Then God appeared to you and showed you the stars of the sky and gave you a promise about the immeasurable number of offspring you would have.

Why do you think God delayed the fulfillment of His promise to Abram?

Abram struggled with the absence of God's presence. He worried. He looked elsewhere for answers. Yet, when God finally spoke, illustrating His promise with a beautiful analogy of the stars in the heavens, Abram "believed in the LORD" (15:6, NASB).

Part of having faith is recognizing that God is always at work, even though He may appear to be silent. How can we respond to express our faith and to open ourselves to the work He wants to do in our character as we wait?

How does God's faithfulness in the past—through biblical stories, stories of people you know, or your own experiences—help you stay faithful during times of God's silence?

In our personal study this week, we will look more deeply into the story of Abram and Sarai and learn what eventually happened.

PRAY

- Begin your prayer time acknowledging God's presence in your group.
- Pray for people in your lives, including members of your group, who are struggling with God's silence.
- Pray that you can each be thoughtful ambassadors for Jesus in your lives.

Read week 1 and complete the activities on the following pages before the next group experience.

Video sessions available for purchase at www.lifeway.com/unanswered

DAY 1

ABRAHAM:
FAITH AND SILENCE

According to the Oxford English Dictionary, *despair* is defined as "complete loss or absence of hope."[1] I think my wife and I reached that point when we wanted to have children but were unable to conceive. For nearly five years we experienced God's deafening silence.

Identify a time in your life (which may be currently) that you have faced a trial, adversity, or God's lingering silence. Now place an *X* on each scale to indicate how you are responding or have responded to it.

JOYFUL	DESPAIRING
CALM	ANGRY
PATIENT	ANXIOUS
COMPOSED	FRANTIC
HOPEFUL	HOPELESS

Would you say your responses were normal, healthy ways to function in difficult, painful circumstances, or do any of these responses reveal areas where you need to grow in trusting God? Why?

In our group time we studied God's renewed promise to Abram as he and Sarai were waiting to conceive the child of promise, and we observed Abram's faithful response (see Gen. 15:1-7). But Sarai wasn't with Abram when he experienced God in Genesis 15. Notwithstanding God's promises, Sarai convinced Abram to allow Hagar to act as a surrogate mother (see 16:1-3), and Ishmael was born to Abram (see v. 15).

Read Genesis 17:1-8,15-22.

As Genesis 17 begins, 13 years have passed since Ishmael was born (see 16:16). We have no other details about what was happening during these years of silence between Genesis 16 and 17. We can only speculate that God left Abram, for a time, to do things his own way—having a child with Hagar instead of waiting for God to enable him and Sarah to have a son—and God stopped speaking to him.

> **When God greeted Abram after years of silence and everything that had occurred in between, why do you think He reminded Abram that He was El Shaddai—"Almighty God" (Gen. 17:1, NKJV)?**

God made a number of promises to Abraham in this passage. A few of these would be fulfilled in Abraham's lifetime, but most were promises for the generations to come, as a result of Abraham's obedience. Throughout these chapters in Genesis, we see Abraham and Sarah trying to resolve their personal concerns and questions, but God had a much bigger picture—a much bigger purpose—in mind. This is a wonderful reminder that our personal obedience and trust in God are blessings not only for our lives but also for generations to come.

Read Genesis 21:1-7.

> **Why God might have waited so long to fulfill His promise?**

As we study the account of Abraham and Sarah, we see that God had much bigger and better plans for and through them than they could even "conceive." They desired a child. God wanted to start a faith movement. They were thinking about the continuance of their family line. God was thinking about the messianic line of Jesus. They were worried about not having an heir. God's concern was for the salvation of all humankind (see Gal. 3:29; Titus 3:7; Jas. 2:5).

> **How does Abraham and Sarah's story help you put your hopes and dreams, as well as God's silence, in perspective?**

In the midst of God's silence and their circumstances, Abram and Sarai turned to human solutions (see Gen. 15:3; 16:2-3) rather than trusting God for His provision. God was asking, "Will you trust Me to love you and keep My covenant promises to you? Do you trust Me to straighten out the mess in your life? Do you trust Me to give you a child?

Do you trust me bring the Savior through your family?" God's plan for the messianic line was to begin with a miraculous birth and end with the even more miraculous birth of Jesus of Nazareth. In spite of his doubts and attempts to get ahead of God, Abraham is cited throughout the New Testament as an example of faith (see Rom. 4:3,9,22; Gal 3:6; Jas. 2:23). God wants us to trust Him. To trust His way as well as His timing.

In December 2007 Audrey and I felt convicted to pray daily for the Lord to work miraculously and allow us to grow our family. We gathered each day and carefully prayed through our struggle. We came to a point of having total peace with God, no matter what He decided. In August 2008 we were on a spiritual retreat and decided to study passages in the Bible related to trusting God.

Early one morning in October of that year, Audrey took a home pregnancy test. Those pregnancy tests had become a reminder of no to us. After five years of no, my wife could barely walk through the aisle of a pharmacy without seeing a home pregnancy test, being reminded that nothing had worked. However, that October morning was different. I remember Audrey running toward me, collapsing in my arms, and saying, "It said yes!" Nine months later, my wife gave birth to our child of promise, Lily Faith (who now also has a little brother, Justin). God reminded us, just as He had reminded Abraham and Sarah, that He is El Shaddai—Almighty God.

These stories remind us that when we cannot see the hand of God, we must trust His heart and character. When I fail to understand why things are going the way they are in my life, I must remember that God sees the end from the beginning, and He wants me to trust Him. Just like Abraham and Sarah.

If you had a friend who had continually asked God for something but had experienced His silence, what would you encourage him or her to do?

Close your time today in prayer, acknowledging that God is sovereign (in control) even when He seems silent to us. Pray, trusting the Lord hears the cries of your heart and knowing He will answer. Meditate on the following verse, thanking God for His love, patience, provision, and power.

Is anything too hard for the LORD?
GENESIS 18:14, NKJV

DAY 2

DEBUNKING THE MYTH

Does your life ever feel as if God has "unfollowed" you because of sin or maybe for unknown reasons? Have you ever sensed that God was playing a game of hide-and-go-seek with you? It is anything but fun. It can even seem to be a cruel, cosmic timeout—a heavenly ignore. God's hiddenness can be isolating, especially when you think God is being silent because of your sin.

But there is a myth to be debunked about God's silence. There is an erroneous understanding among many Christians that God's silence always equals His chastisement in our lives. *Chastisement* is a word we rarely hear in modern churches, but it is found in the Bible. Chastisement is the experience of God's discipline in our lives. God's silence and God's chastisement are very different things and certainly are not synonymous. If God is silent toward us, it does not always mean that He is disciplining us.

In Psalm 66 David suggested that God would not listen to his prayers because of sin, but this sin referred to the potential of specific, unresolved sin in David's heart (see v. 18). We all sin, so we must constantly search our hearts for unresolved sin, repent of that sin, and rest in God's promise that He is working for our ultimate good (see Rom. 8:28). Then we can affirm with David:

> God has surely listened
>   and has heard my prayer.
> Praise be to God,
>   who has not rejected my prayer
>   or withheld his love from me!
> **PSALM 66:19-20, NIV**

On the other hand, when God is silent, we must not assume that the cause is our sin. Recall the episode in John's Gospel in which Jesus saw a blind man and His own disciples questioned Jesus about the cause of the man's suffering:

> As he passed by, he saw a man blind from birth. And his disciples asked him, "Rabbi, who sinned, this man or his parents, that he was born blind?" Jesus answered, "It was not that this man sinned, or his parents, but that the works of God might be displayed in him.
> **JOHN 9:1-3, ESV**

Jewish families in the first century who suffered with handicaps, birth defects, or special needs were considered outcasts. I am sure they felt that God was distant. However, as we learn in John 9, God had a greater plan for this particular family to experience the power of God with healing and deliverance (see vv. 6-7). It is incorrect to view every case of God's silence as discipline for sin.

In what ways are God's discipline and God's silence different?

When you have experienced a time of God's silence, what did you attribute that silence to?

If you are experiencing the silence of God, do not believe the lie that you are a second-tier, second-rate Christian. In reality, it is possible, even probable, that it means quite the opposite. God has entrusted you with His apparent silence for a greater reason. When you sense God's silence, trust is the central issue that needs your focus. Will you trust God to straighten out this mess in your life? Will you trust Him to see you through the desert? Will you trust Him, even when He says no, wait, or not now?

What are three things in your life right now that you need to submit and trust in God for?

1.

2.

3.

The Bible is a time machine, a portal to the historical past, providing access to examples of common men and women who transcended extremely difficult moments with profound courage and faith. As we search the Scriptures for answers to the unanswered questions, we must remember that the Bible is history, not mythology. The stories of the Bible reflect the real world in which they took place. Have you considered that God's silence is biblical? Casual readers of the Bible are often surprised to learn that several major Bible characters faced moments of deafening silence from God.

A CASE STUDY OF JOSEPH

Consider Joseph's experience with the silence of God. Joseph was obedient to God; he trusted, obeyed, and followed, yet he ended up in a foreign land, Egypt, a teenage victim, sold in a human-trafficking transaction to become a slave in Potiphar's house. Joseph was wrongly accused, and Potiphar had Joseph thrown into an Egyptian prison. Joseph's suffering is captured in this portion of Psalm 105:

> … Joseph, who was sold as a slave.
> They hurt his feet with shackles;
> his neck was put in an iron collar.
> Until the time his prediction came true,
> the word of the LORD tested him.
> **PSALM 105:17-19, HCSB**

Genesis 40 concludes by saying Joseph was forgotten in prison. God was silent. The bigger story was that God did not want Joseph to remain in the land of Canaan, where his family would have most likely died in the coming famine. God did not want Joseph to remain as a slave in Potiphar's house either. God wanted Joseph to be Pharaoh's prisoner. Why? Because God wanted to favor him in the eyes of Pharaoh. God's silence was a test. Joseph's transformation to becoming the second most powerful man in Egypt happened through a period of God's silence.

■HENRY BLACKABY ON THE SILENCE OF GOD

I went through a lengthy time when God was silent. … I did not frantically search for an answer but continued my daily reading of God's Word. I was convinced that as I regularly read the Word of God, the Spirit of God—who knew the mind of God for me—was in the process of helping me understand what God was doing in my life. God will let you know what He is doing in your life when and if you need to know.[2]

When I pray and God is silent, I still pray through my sin checklist. Sometimes God's silences are caused by sin in my life. If unconfessed sin is in my life, I confess it and make it right. If God is still silent after that, I get ready for a new experience with Him I have never previously experienced. Sometimes God is silent as He prepares to bring you to a deeper understanding of Himself. Sometimes His silence is designed to bring me into a state of absolute dependence on and trust in God. Whenever God is silent, continue doing the last thing God told you and watch and wait for a fresh encounter with Him.[3]

What might Joseph have learned during his imprisonment? About himself? About God?

God uses this time of waiting to prepare us to receive the plans and tasks He has for us. He is refining our character and forging stronger reliance on and faith in Him so that we will be prepared for what He wants us to do.

Remember that you are not alone in the stillness. You are in good company. When you realize that Abraham, Joseph, and many of the great prophets all persevered and were eventually promoted through God's silence, you recognize that you are not alone. You are not the first Christian facing the juxtaposition of maturing in your faith yet sensing that God is further from you. The reality is God's silence is real, biblical, personal, common, and not always a bad thing. This principle is not something I learned in a seminar; rather, it was reality for me and my beloved wife.

These stories remind us that when we cannot see the hand of God, we must trust in His heart and character. When we fail to understand why things are going the way they are in our lives, we must remember that God sees the end from the beginning, and He wants us to trust Him.

Close your study time in prayer. Ask God to reveal unrepentant sin in your life that needs to resolved. Express your willingness to place your full trust in Him. Ask God to draw you closer to Him, especially in a times of trial and confusion.

DAY 3

WHAT TO DO WHILE YOU WAIT, PART 1

Two themes quickly rise to the surface when we read Paul's letters: (1) the trials that brought him physical and emotional pain, perplexity, and sorrow and (2) the encouragement and strength God gave him during his time of waiting. In fact, Paul was able to thank God for his trials, rejoice in them, and use the lessons he learned to encourage others.

> **How could your perspective on trials and silence affect the way you respond to them?**

We can learn much from the life of the apostle Paul about how to live so that when difficulties and silence come our way, God can position us to experience a transformed life as we wait.

Read Acts 20:13-17.

Paul decided to stay at Troas while his companions sailed around Cape Lectum. He arranged for them to pick him up at Assos because he wanted to walk the 20-mile journey alone. Why would he do this? Paul needed time with God alone before this strategic meeting with the leaders of Ephesus. Paul loved the Lord and wanted to spend time alone with Him. If you tend to rush from one Sunday to the next without making time to be alone with the Lord, you are missing something in your life. Frankly, sometimes the answer to the question "What do I do when God is silent?" is to get away from the noise and spend time alone with God, listening to Him through the Word and prayer.

> **How much interaction do you typically have with God while waiting?**

> **How will you apply the example of Paul's commitment to spend more time in solitude with God? Prayerfully record a plan for how, when, and where you will spend time with God.**

Paul had spent three years in Ephesus, and he wanted to meet with the leaders of that church. In the interest of time, Paul sailed past Ephesus and asked the leaders to meet him at Miletus, 30 miles south of Ephesus. This address to the Ephesian elders is the only sermon in Acts addressed to a Christian audience and, as such, is the most similar to the teachings in Paul's epistles. The sermon is unique in that it reveals Paul the caring pastor rather than Paul the bold evangelist or ardent defender of the faith.

> Read Acts 20:18-19. From what you know about Paul and have seen in these verses, how would you describe Paul's heart and character? What inspired him? What was important to him? What kept him going?

In these two verses we discover the first 3 of 12 principles drawn from Acts 20 for continuing to live for God and serve Him while undergoing trials or waiting for Him to speak or act in our lives (You will study the other 9 tomorrow).

1. BE AN EXAMPLE: "You know how I lived the whole time I was with you" (v. 18, NIV). There was no question how Paul lived. His life was above reproach; it was an open book to these men. He didn't say to them, "You know how I spoke" or "You know all the accolades I gained." He said, "You know how I lived." Our commitment to Christ is an example to others when we wait or suffer for Him.

> In what ways can you be an example to others in the midst of your waiting?

2. SERVE HUMBLY: "I served the Lord with great humility" (v. 19, NIV). Paul used the word *douleúo*, which means *slave*, to express the idea "When I came to Ephesus, I served as a slave to Jesus Christ." What do slaves do? They immediately, unquestioningly obey the master. Seventeen times in his letters Paul wrote that he was a slave of Jesus Christ. This was an important indication of the way Paul saw his relationship with the Master.

Paul had served "with great humility" in a world in which humility was deemed to be a fault, not a virtue—a quality befitting only a slave. Even in a time of waiting, Paul continued to humbly serve the Lord and the churches.

> What can you do to follow Paul's example by being a humble servant (slave) of Jesus?

3. SERVE WITH PASSION: "I served the Lord … with tears" (v. 19, NIV). Paul experienced God's silence with many tears, as he described in his letters:

> I wrote you out of great distress and anguish of
> heart and with many tears, not to grieve you but
> to let you know the depth of my love for you.
> **2 CORINTHIANS 2:4, NIV**

> As I have often told you before and now tell you again
> even with tears, many live as enemies of the cross of Christ.
> **PHILIPPIANS 3:18, NIV**

The Corinthians had written Paul about all the problems in their church. As he wrote back to them, tears christened his response. Yet he continued serving because he considered the gospel more important than trying to escape suffering or personal discomfort.

Until our hearts are broken for lost people, we will never be able to reach them. Until people sense the love of God in us, they will never respond to the love of God we describe.

■ WHEN GOD'S SILENCE IS CONFUSING

When you face confusing circumstances, don't blame God. Don't give up following Him. Go to God. Ask Him to reveal the truth of your circumstances. Ask Him to show you His perspective. Then wait on the Lord.[4] You cannot know the truth of your circumstance until you have heard from God.[5]

Even as you wait for God to speak or act, you can focus your heart and mind in these ways to hear from Him.

1. Settle in your mind that God has forever demonstrated His unfailing love for you on the cross. That love will never change.
2. Do not try to understand what God is like from the middle of your circumstances.
3. Go to God and ask Him to help you see His perspective on your situation.
4. Wait on the Holy Spirit. He may take God's Word and help you understand your circumstances.
5. Adjust your life to God and to what you see Him doing in your circumstances.
6. Do all He tells you to do.
7. Experience God working in and through you to accomplish His purposes.[6]

Take a moment to examine your heart. Even if you are personally experiencing God's silence, God desires for you to be an example, to serve humbly, and to serve with passion. Think about the people who live near you or the people you work with. Does it ever cross your mind where they will spend eternity? Think of one person or group of people you know who do not have a relationship with Jesus as their Savior. Write a prayer for them below. I encourage you to personalize it with a first name. Simply pour out your heart to God for them and how He wants you to be an example for them and to serve them.

DAY 4

WHAT TO DO WHILE YOU WAIT, PART 2

Yesterday you studied the first 3 of 12 principles drawn from Acts 20 for living in obedience while you wait on God. Today you will examine the last 9.

Read Acts 20:20-38.

How would you describe the tone of Paul's remarks?

What were Paul's priorities, according to these verses?

4. BE COMMITTED TO TRUTH: "I have not hesitated to preach anything that would be helpful to you" (v. 20, NIV). Paul came to Ephesus, with all the decadence and occultism in that city, and instead of trying to fit in, he simply asked God to give him strength and power to confront that culture with God's love. Paul had a total, not a partial, commitment to truth. Are we committed in whole, not in part, to the truth of God's Word? We cannot pick and choose what we like about God's message and what we do not.

> Record a couple of ways you can teach the truth to people by your words and actions in your circumstances.

5. DO NOT COMPROMISE: "I have declared to both Jews and Greeks that they must turn to God in repentance and have faith in our Lord Jesus" (v. 21, NIV). The arrangement of the words in the Greek text presents a vital lesson: we will never have repentance without faith, and we will never have faith without repentance. Think of the prodigal son's father, who rejoiced that his son had returned (see Luke 15:22-24). The Hebrew word *teshuva*[7] means *to return*. Paul never compromised that message of returning to God.

When people believe in Jesus Christ, He will change the way they live. And when He changes the way they live, they will grow in their faith in Him. Our goal as the church is to make people true disciples whose spiritual maturity is evident.

6. PERSEVERE: "Now, compelled by the Spirit, I am going to Jerusalem" (v. 22, NIV). The word *compelled* refers to physical binding with chains and ropes. Paul was "bound" in his spirit to fulfill the ministry God had called him to do. What waited for him in Jerusalem? Paul understood that imprisonment, persecution, and even death were possible. Yet he was not afraid.

If we are going to be faithful to God even during His silence, we must learn how to persevere. Trials will come. Perseverance will energize us to transcend those trials.

7. BE COURAGEOUS IN THE FACE OF ADVERSITY: "The Holy Spirit warns me that prison and hardships are facing me" (v. 23, NIV). We've all had difficulties in life, but have you ever been physically persecuted for your faith? Have you ever been beaten as Paul was in Acts 16:22? Have you ever been publicly maligned or put in prison for two years? Yet in spite of all Paul had been through, he was undeterred. It was as if he were saying, "I cannot wait to go to Jerusalem; I must finish my ministry."

Think of a time that you have waited on God. How was courage needed during that experience?

8. HAVE THE RIGHT ATTITUDE: "I consider my life worth nothing to me; my only aim is to … complete the task the Lord Jesus has given me—the task of testifying to the good news of God's grace" (v. 24, NIV). Paul's attitude was: Jesus first; everything else, second. Until we emulate this attitude, this mind of Christ, see Phil. 2:1-18), we will not allow Christ to be preeminent in our lives.

Use Paul's statement as a prompt to write your own life statement, specific to you and your circumstances.

"I _____ [your name] consider my life worth" … (list what your life entails):

"… nothing to me; my only aim is to … complete the task the Lord Jesus has given to me" (record the task[s] the Lord has given you to accomplish):

Read your statement aloud. Do you have trouble believing any of this statement? Why or why not?

9. COMMIT TO FINISH STRONG: "My only aim is to finish the race and complete the task the Lord Jesus has given me" (v. 24, NIV). A great start is no guarantee of a great finish. There are too many shooting-star Christians. We must pray for greater resolve and long-term faithfulness to wait on the Lord and follow through with what He wants you to do.

10. BE RESPONSIBLE; PROTECT THE SHEEP UNDER YOUR CARE: "Keep watch over yourselves and all the flock. … I know that after I leave, savage wolves will come in among you and will not spare the flock. Even from your own number men will arise and distort the truth in order to draw away disciples after them" (vv. 28-30, NIV). These wolves were coming from inside, not from outside, the church. Paul founded this church, and yet he warned its leaders that these wolves would come from "among you" (v. 29, NIV). Take responsibility for the things God has given you to do even if you are waiting.

11. DO NOT QUIT: "Remember that for three years I never stopped warning each of you night and day with tears" (v. 31, NIV). Paul had said in verse 26, "I am innocent of the blood of any of you" (NIV). Paul could leave a city of approximately 250,000 and know he had presented the gospel to every single one of them. That was an effective ministry!

How are you tempted to quit while waiting for God to speak or act?

12. PRAY AND LOVE: "When Paul had finished speaking, he knelt down with all of them and prayed. They all wept as they embraced him and kissed him" (vv. 36-37, NIV). This is the kind of love that needs to characterize our families and churches. Our pastors and our people should sense this kind of love. Seventeen times the New Testament instructs us to "love one another" or "love each other."

What do you sense God has asked you to do in response to the past two days of study? What will be required to do it? What would you be willing to give up to complete it?

Response:

Requirements:

Willing to give up:

The founding pastor of the Ephesian church was Paul, its second pastor was Timothy, and its third pastor was the apostle John. Yet in Revelation 2:4 we learn that the Christians in Ephesus had lost their first love, their love for Christ. It is vital for the church today to heed this passage. You are still responsible for showing Christ's character and for being on mission even as you wait on God.

Review the 12 principles for staying faithful to God while you wait for Him to act. Circle or highlight the ones you most need to work on. Then pray that you and your group will be obedient in these ways.

DAY 5

LIVING FOR GOD OVER A LIFETIME, EVEN WHEN HE IS SILENT

Begin today's lesson by reading and reflecting on Jesus' words:

Ask and it will be given to you; seek and you will find;
knock and the door will be opened to you. For everyone
who asks receives; the one who seeks finds; and to
the one who knocks, the door will be opened.
MATTHEW 7:7-8, NIV

How do Jesus' words resonate with you when God seems silent?

All three verbs—*ask, seek,* and *knock*—are in the present tense: keep asking, keep seeking, keep knocking. Most important, keep trusting God, no matter what. Jesus was not giving us a magic formula as if He were a genie in a bottle; He was teaching us how to live a consistent, persistent life of faith and total dependence on God.

One of the Bible's best models of this kind of life is Daniel. When Daniel was a young man, he was taken from his home in Jerusalem against his will when King Nebuchadnezzar forced him to move to Babylon, a very evil, decadent city that was filled with idols to false gods, sexual deviance, and human sacrifice.

When the Jews were finally able to return to Jerusalem, Daniel was apparently too old to travel back. According to tradition, Daniel died and was buried outside Babylon. After all of Daniel's years of faithfulness, he was not able to return to his homeland, but apparently, that hope was not what had driven him. He had lived a principled, God-centered life while he waited on God's deliverance, both for him and for the nation.

The Book of Daniel is composed of 12 chapters, and each one contains an important principle that reveals how Daniel was able to overcome his circumstances and transcend his trials as he waited on God.

Read the following verses from each of the 12 chapters of the Book of Daniel, along with the principles they reveal. Prayerfully note anything you sense God wants you to focus on, do, or change as you wait for Him to speak or act.

DANIEL 1:8 Absolute resolve: I have made up my mind.

DANIEL 2:17-19,26-28 God is my ultimate source of insight and understanding.

DANIEL 3:8-12 I can expect opposition and harassment when I do God's will.

DANIEL 4:13 Because of His love for us, God has angels who watch over us.

DANIEL 5:1-4 I will always stay in control of my actions.

DANIEL 6:4 My life work will be marked by integrity.

DANIEL 7:28 When overwhelmed, I will go to God first and others later.

DANIEL 8:27 My faith will never be an excuse not to give my employer or family my very best effort.

DANIEL 9:23 I can change things in heaven and on earth by my prayers.

DANIEL 10:12 When I meet the qualifications, I know God will grant endless blessings to me.

DANIEL 11:35 Nobody knows my future better or understands my needs more clearly than God.

DANIEL 12:12-13 God will give me a great inheritance someday because of my faithfulness.

Daniel 12:12-13, the last two verses of the book, contain a vital principle for Christians: we must be faithful to God as we wait for Him to complete His work in our lives. In fact, the Bible describes us as a people who wait:

If we hope for what we do not
yet have, we wait for it patiently.
ROMANS 8:25, NIV

I remain confident of this:
    I will see the goodness of the LORD
    in the land of the living.
Wait for the LORD;
    be strong and take heart
    and wait for the LORD.
PSALM 27:13-14, NIV

What do these verses teach you about what to do and how to live when God is silent?

When you struggle with God's apparent silence, you are in very good company. King David wrote:

My God, my God, why have you forsaken me?
    Why are you so far from saving me,
    so far from my cries of anguish?
My God, I cry out by day, but you do not answer,
    by night, but I find no rest.
PSALM 22:1-2, NIV

The first part of that passage may sound familiar. Jesus spoke those words from the cross as He took our sins on Himself (see Matt. 27:46). Read David's next statement:

Yet you are enthroned as the Holy One;
    you are the one Israel praises.
In you our ancestors put their trust;
    they trusted and you delivered them.
PSALM 22:3-4, NIV

David turned from focusing on his own difficulties and his questions about God's silence to trusting and praising God for who He is and what He had already done.

How can worshiping God and recalling His provision in the past help you understand God's silence and maintain a faithful perspective?

We generally see our lives from a limited point of view. God has an eternal perspective on everything that happens in His universe. As we have seen this week, our best response—actually, our only response—is to trust Him.

> List names of people you know who are experiencing God's silence. Ask God to help you listen and respond in a winsome, attractive way as a thoughtful ambassador of Jesus.

Close your time in this study by praising God for His lovingkindness and power. Express your trust in Him even though you may not have all the answers you want. Thank Him for being present with you right now. Ask for His strength as you keep asking, keep seeking Him, and keep knocking. Finally, read Revelation 3:19-22 and hear Jesus' appeal and promise to you.

■ ENGAGEMENT PRINCIPLES

Here are five important principles for engaging in a conversation about tough questions of faith. We will focus on a different principle at the end of each week of this study to stimulate ideas for engaging people with the love of God and the truth of His Word.

1. SHUT UP AND LISTEN. To guide someone to the truth, you must be a great listener. Remember, your goal is not to win a debate at all costs but to build the foundation of a trusting relationship through which you can show compassion and share biblical truth when the person is ready to hear it.

2. AVOID ISLAND FEVER. To engage, you must get out of your comfort zone.

3. BE COOL. The more you know, the more relaxed you should be.

4. BE CURIOUS. Ask questions; allow the other person to be an "expert." Being smart does not mean you think others are stupid.

5. DON'T GO BEAST MODE. Learn how to answer tough questions in a winsome way as a thoughtful ambassador for Christ.

BODY OF PROOF

WHY CAN WE TRUST IN THE BODILY RESURRECTION OF JESUS?

JOHN 19:29

that the Scripture might be fulfilled, He said, "I'm thirsty!" ²⁹ A jar full of sour wine was sitting there; so they fixed a sponge full of sour wine on hyssop and held it up to His mouth.
ᵃ Ps 69:21

³⁰ When Jesus had received the sour wine, He said, ᵃ"It is finished!" Then bowing His head, He ᵇgave up His spirit.
ᵃ Jn 17:4 ᵇ Php 2:8

Jesus' Side Pierced

ᵃSince it was the preparation day, the Jews ᵇdid not want the bodies to remain on the cross on the Sabbath (that Sabbath was ᶜa special day). requested that Pilate have the legs broken and that their bodies taken away. ³² So the soldiers and broke the legs of the first and of the other one who had crucified with Him. ³³ When they they did not break His the law at He was already of the soldiers with a spear, and at once blood and water came out. ³⁵ ᵉHe who has testified so that you also believe. His testimony is true, and he is telling the truth. ³⁶ For these things happened ᶠso that the Scripture would be fulfilled: Not one of His bones will be broken. ³⁷ Also, another Scripture says: ᵍThey will look at the One they pierced.
ᵃ Mk 15:42 ᵇ Dt 21:23 ᶜ Ex 12:18
ᵈ Zch 13:1 ᵉ Jn 20:31; 1Jn 1:1
ᶠ Ex 12:46; Ps 34:20 ᵍ Zch 12:10

After this, Joseph of Arimathea, who was a disciple cretly ᵇbecause of his fear of the Jews—asked Pilate that he might remove Jesus' body. Pilate gave him permission, so he came and took His body away. ³⁹ Nicodemus (who had previ-

ously come to Him at night) also came, bringing a mixture of about 75 pounds of myrrh and aloes. ⁴⁰ Then they took Jesus' body and wrapped it in linen cloths with the aromatic spices, according to the burial custom of the Jews. ⁴¹ There was a garden in the place where He was crucified. A ᵈnew tomb was in the garden; no one had yet been placed in it. ⁴² ᵉThey placed Jesus there because of the Jewish preparation and since the tomb was nearby.
ᵃ Mt 27:57 ᵇ Pr 29:25 ᶜ Jn 3:1-2
ᵈ Mt 27:60; Lk 23:53 ᵉ Is 53:9

The Empty Tomb

20 On the ᵃfirst day of the week ᵇMary Magdalene came to the tomb early, while it was still dark. She saw that the stone had been removed from the tomb. ² So she ran to Simon Peter and to the ᵇother disciple, the one Jesus loved, and said to them, "They have taken the Lord out of the tomb, and we don't know where they have put Him!"
ᵃ Mt 28:1 ᵇ Jn 13:23

³ At that, ᵃPeter and the other disciple went out, heading for the tomb. ⁴ The two were running together, but the other disciple outran Peter and got to the tomb first. ⁵ Stooping down, he saw ᵇthe linen cloths lying there, yet he did not go in. ⁶ Then, following him, Simon Peter came also. He entered the tomb and saw the linen cloths lying there. ⁷ The wrapping that had been on His head was not lying with the linen cloths but was folded up in a separate place by itself. ⁸ The tomb first; then he saw and believed. ⁹ For they still did not understand the ᵃScripture that He must rise from the dead. ¹⁰ Then the disciples went home again.
ᵃ Lk 24:12 ᵇ Jn 19:40
ᶜ Ps 16:10; Mt 16:21

START

Is it possible that one morning changed the world? Could most, if not all, of life's problems be answered by an unusual occurrence on a Sunday morning in April A.D. 30?[1] Could it be that God's answer to the injustice in our world is exactly what happened over a 39-hour period at a Jewish criminal's borrowed tomb in a Roman outpost? Could it be so simple?

In a word, yes. The resurrection of Jesus Christ is the seminal issue for the church today, even as it was that first Easter in the first century. There is nothing more important for a Christian than Jesus' resurrection. Yet it assumes a heavy burden of proof.

What were your family's Easter traditions when you were a child?

How much do you know about the facts, evidence, and implications of Jesus' resurrection?

How well do you think you could answer a skeptic's questions about the resurrection?

Unfortunately, the most important fact of the Christian faith is also the most misunderstood. Most followers of Jesus have a woefully inadequate understanding of Jesus' resurrection. In our session today, we will try to change that.

WATCH

1. We must recover a resurrection-centric faith.

2. We need to refresh our minds with the evidence for a resurrection-centric faith.

3. I must recommit to live the mission of resurrection faith now and be resurrection-centric with all the problems and difficulties of my life.

RESPOND

What one truth from Jeremiah's teaching resonated most with you?

It is important to understand that in the world of Jesus and the early church, belief in resurrection from the dead was mocked and attacked by thinkers throughout the Roman Empire. If the disciples wanted to create or invent a new religion, they could not have selected a more confusing place to start than imagining a story of a decomposing corpse coming to life. The early Christian movement should have died. But it did not. Why? Its founder was alive.

Read 1 Corinthians 15:1-8,12-20.

Based on this passage alone, if someone asked you to explain what the gospel is, how would you respond?

In what ways are Jesus' death, burial, and resurrection good news for you?

There is no passage in the entire Bible that we should take more seriously than 1 Corinthians 15:3-8. The apostle Paul tells us that the matter of Jesus' bodily resurrection was a matter of "first importance" (v. 3, NIV).

Understanding this passage is the key to understanding the theology of Paul and the entire New Testament. This early passage also answers skeptics who claim that the resurrection story of Jesus is a fable created in the years and decades after His death.

What proof did Paul give that Jesus' resurrection really happened?

Identify the various people who witnessed Jesus' resurrection. Why was it important that their stories corroborated one another's—that they all testified to the same thing?

The Greco-Roman culture of the first century did not understand why anyone would believe that a body came back to life. The proclamation of the early Christian leaders—that a ripe corpse came back to life—would have been disgusting and strange to any Roman. This is most likely why Paul was mocked on Mars Hill for proclaiming the resurrection (see Acts 17:32). N. T. Wright drives this point home:

> The immediate conclusion is clear. Christianity was born into a world where its central claim was known to be false. Many believed that the dead were non-existent; outside Judaism, nobody believed in resurrection.[2]

What objections to the resurrection do people raise today?

In what way does the resurrection give us an eternal hope in our salvation from sin and guilt?

In our personal study this week, we will investigate Jesus' resurrection and ours more deeply. We will look at ways the resurrection affects our lives as Christ followers, both in the here and now and in eternity.

PRAY

- Begin your prayer time by acknowledging the presence of Jesus as you meet together, something that is possible only because of His resurrection.
- Spend a few moments giving praise to Jesus, who gave us victory over sin and death through His death and resurrection.
- Pray that you will be ready to respond effectively to questions about the resurrection.

Read week 2 and complete the activities on the following pages before the next group experience.

Video sessions available for purchase at www.lifeway.com/unanswered

DAY 1

THE MOST EPIC
WEEKEND EVER

Travel back in time with me to that April day in first-century Jerusalem. There is a solid evidential basis to date Jesus' resurrection on Friday, April 7, A.D. 30. The forecast would have called for warm weather. The city of Jerusalem would have been brimming over with Jews who had ascended to the city for the annual Passover festival.

Matthew 28:1-10 is a familiar Bible passage for many people. Take a moment to read these verses. As you study, what are some details you never noticed before?

All four Gospel writers tell us it was women—the same women who had supported Jesus during his earthly ministry (see Luke 8:1-3)—who first witnessed the empty tomb. In the first-century world, women were not viewed as trustworthy, so they would have been considered unreliable first witnesses of such a monumental event.

Since women were not viewed as trustworthy, do you think it makes the witnessing of an empty tomb more likely or less likely? Why or why not?

The Gospel writers did not make up this story out of thin air. If they had, they would not have used women as the most credible first witnesses to the empty tomb.

History also tells us that something happened to Jesus on that first Sunday morning. Something happened that changed the lives of the people who witnessed these events. Friday night the disciples were running scared. A few days later, they were more than willing to endure ridicule, imprisonment, mistreatment, and even death for what they had seen.

Read Acts 4:1-3,18-20.

What do you make of Peter and John's bold statement in verse 20?

The Sadducees were a Jewish sect that did not believe in resurrection, so they were upset by what the disciples were teaching the people. This incident is the first recorded experience in the early church when believers faced persecution from the religious leaders, but it would not be the last. Over the years believers faced many threats; imprisonments; beatings; and ultimately, death. And all this was based on the claim of Jesus' resurrection.

> **How do you explain the courage of Peter and John, as well as the other followers of Christ, in the face of persecution and even possible death?**

Was Jesus really raised from the dead? How do we know for sure? What evidence has the most explanatory power? What is the best evidence for His resurrection? Was resurrection just an educated guess on the part of the New Testament authors? Did the disciples steal the body?

How we answer those questions changes everything. As followers of Jesus, we have to prepare ourselves to explain that Jesus' resurrection is not a myth, a legend, or a fairytale but a historical fact.

The resurrection is a controversial subject today, even among Christians. And for many of our non-Christian neighbors, Easter means nothing more than chocolate rabbits, decorated eggs, and perhaps a corsage for Grandma. One newspaper headlined, "Easter Sunday Is the Super Bowl of Church Attendance,"[3] and yet

■ EVIDENCE FOR JESUS' RESURRECTION

1. The story of the empty tomb is found in all four Gospels and is implicit in the early church's proclamation of the resurrection. How would they preach the bodily resurrection of Jesus if everyone in Jerusalem knew that His body was still in the tomb?
2. It is difficult to believe that the early church would have fabricated the story of the resurrection and then made women the first witnesses to the empty tomb and the resurrection, since women were not considered reliable witnesses in Jewish culture.
3. Something incredible must have taken place on that Sunday to cause Jewish believers to begin worshiping on the first day of the week instead of the Sabbath (see Acts 20:7; 1 Cor. 16:2; Rev. 1:10).
4. Nothing short of the miracle of the resurrection can explain the postresurrection transformation in the disciples. The biblical record indicates that at the time of Jesus' arrest, they all fled (see Mark 14:50). When the women reported that they had seen Jesus, the men did not believe (see Luke 24:11). Yet these same men were later willing to suffer persecution and martyrdom in order to preach Jesus as the resurrected Lord.[4]

few Christians are able to give a reasonable answer for why they know Jesus rose from the grave. They are unable to offer any real evidence. Like the early believers, the resurrection is central to our faith. As Paul stated in 1 Corinthians 15, if Jesus was not raised from the dead, our faith is useless (see v. 14). It is futile; we are still swallowed up in our sins (see v. 17).

Read the following verses from your Bible. If Jesus had not been raised from the dead, how would it affect what the Bible says in the following passages?

John 11:25-26

Romans 4:23-25

Romans 8:11

Romans 10:9

Based on these verses, how would your faith be affected if there were no resurrection?

In 1 Corinthians 15:55-57, in his discussion about the reality of our belief in the resurrection, the apostle Paul quoted from the Old Testament prophet Hosea:

Where, O death, is your victory?
Where, O death, is your sting? …

Thanks be to God! He gives us the victory
through our Lord Jesus Christ.
1 CORINTHIANS 15:55-57, NIV

Conclude your study time today by reflecting on the truth and power of the resurrection. Thank God for His victory over death and the victory you have through Jesus Christ. Pour out your heart to God in thanksgiving for the power of His resurrection.

DAY 2

THE IMPORTANCE
OF THE PREDICTIONS

Did you know that Jesus predicted His death and resurrection? Jesus' predictions of His death and resurrection provided His followers the foundation for understanding what was to take place. Without Jesus' predictions the disciples would have been left wondering about the whole point of His ministry. Judas Iscariot never saw the resurrected Christ. He had decided to quit following Jesus and give up, probably because he was disillusioned. Judas desired a conqueror. He did not understand Jesus' kingdom message and ministry.

Throughout the Gospels the disciples struggled to understand the true purpose of Jesus' ministry. They expected the Romans to be driven out of Israel; a corrupt, abusive high priesthood to be overthrown; and Jerusalem to be purged. These were messianic expectations that many Jews held to. The Messiah would be a conqueror; He would vanquish the Jewish enemies and restore Jerusalem to its glory.

Read Mark 14:1-10.

> Imagine you are one of Jesus' disciples as you witness this occurrence. Remember your expectations of the Messiah. Consider the commitment you made to Him. As you watch this scene and hear Jesus' words about His burial, what would be going through your mind?

Judas's decision to betray Jesus was confirmed when the woman anointed Jesus' head. Instead of responding, "Yes, this is my messianic anointing. Yes, with God's help we will overthrow the Romans," Jesus said, "She has anointed my body beforehand for burial" (v. 8, ESV). For Judas, this was the last straw.

This event also greatly influenced the rest of the disciples, so Jesus knew He must instruct them. That's the point of His words at the last supper:

> Take it; this is my body. ... This is my blood
> of the covenant, which is poured out for many.
> **MARK 14:22-24, NIV**

Few words of Jesus are as familiar as those He uttered at the last supper with His disciples. Then, according to the tradition passed down to the apostle Paul, Jesus added, "Do this in remembrance of me" (1 Cor. 11:24-25, NIV). The words of Jesus clearly allude to Exodus 24:8:

> This is the blood of the covenant that the LORD has made with you in accordance with all these words.
> **EXODUS 24:8, NIV**

The new covenant that people talked about had been promised in Jeremiah 31:31:

> Behold, the days are coming, declares the Lord, when I will make a new covenant with the house of Israel and the house of Judah.
> **JEREMIAH 31:31, ESV**

Jesus was predicting and heralding a new covenant that would be related to the Sinai covenant of shed blood, when Moses had said, "This is the blood of the covenant" (Ex. 24:8, NIV). Jesus took the two Old Testament covenants and merged them together in His own death and resurrection. He would be that sacrifice. Atonement would not be through the blood of bulls and goats but through His own blood.

Jesus' words at the last supper laid the groundwork so that when the disciples were stunned a few days later by the empty tomb and the resurrection appearances, they would be able to look back and understand that Jesus' death was not a disruption; rather, it furthered the kingdom proclamation. The words of institution redefined and reempowered their mission, their proclamation of a Messiah who in fact would save them—but not by killing Romans. Instead, Jesus' death and resurrection defeated the ultimate enemies of all humans: sin and death.

Jesus' words provided His disciples (including us) the theological context for understanding the significance of the resurrection. Without Jesus' passion predictions, the disciples would have been very confused about the point of Jesus' ministry. Jesus' death and resurrection were a consummation of God's saving work, His redeeming work for all humanity. And so they were a proclamation of His continuing ministry to advance the kingdom of God but now clearly focused on the redemption of the entire world.

The risen Jesus then told His disciples to go out and make disciples of the nations. Of all peoples. Not just Israel:

You will receive power when the Holy Spirit has
come upon you; and you shall be My witnesses
both in Jerusalem, and in all Judea and Samaria,
and even to the remotest part of the earth.
ACTS 1:8, NASB

It was Israel's story, but, as the promises to the prophets and patriarchs hinted
at, it was going to be life-changing for the entire world, a blessing for the whole
world, not simply the exaltation of a single people at the expense of Gentile
neighbors. It would be a redeeming, restorative, redemptive ministry that would
affect the entire planet and in the end would reverse and cure the negative
consequence of humankind's sin and fall.

We partake in the Lord's Supper to remember and proclaim the Lord's death
until He comes again (see 1 Cor. 11:26). But we can also reflect on His resurrection, proclaiming the fact that He lives. Jesus brought the Lord's Supper in the
upper room to a conclusion with these words:

I tell you, I will not drink from this fruit of the
vine from now on until that day when I drink it
new with you in my Father's kingdom.
MATTHEW 26:29

Take a moment and reflect on Jesus' promise that you will someday
commune with Him, your risen Savior, in heaven. How will this realization
affect the way you partake in the Lord's Supper while on earth?

If the early church had a hashtag, it would have been *#onthethirdday*. These words
were critical for the earliest witnesses of the resurrection. They were the most important
words in Christian origins and in the early church (see Acts 10:40 and 1 Cor. 15:4).
In the eighth century B.C the prophet Hosea had used those words to console a
defeated Northern Kingdom with the promise that God would restore the nation:

After two days he will revive us;
    on the third day he will raise us up,
    that we may live before him.
HOSEA 6:2, ESV

Read the following passages. Record the recurring themes and words in each. What message does Scripture reveal in these prophecies?

Mark 8:31

Mark 9:31

Mark 10:33-34

Luke 24:46

Jesus' prediction of His resurrection on the third day was certainly significant to the early church. How is it significant to you and your witness that Jesus' prophecy came true?

As you close today's study, think about what it would have been like to be among the 11 disciples proceeding up the mount of Jesus' ascension in Matthew 28. The text says:

When they saw Him, they worshiped
Him; but some were doubtful.
MATTHEW 28:17, NASB

The word *doubt* or *doubtful (distazo)* in that verse means *to waiver, hesitate, and lack confidence.*

> Where are you today on the mount of ascension? Are you worshiping, or are you doubtful? List any specific doubts you have about the resurrection. Be intentional about seeking answers to those questions this week.

How did Jesus respond when some worshiped and others doubted? He told them, "Go therefore and make disciples of all the nations" (Matt. 28:19, NASB).

Jesus met His followers right where they were—some worshiping and others doubting—and put them on mission. You can be used by God and actively serve Him while you negotiate the doubts in your faith. Doubts don't sideline you. Some days you're on the mountain, seeing the resurrected Jesus and worshiping Him, and other days you find yourself doubting. God still has a plan for you, which is to go and be used. He will be with you, as Jesus has promised.

Close your study time by praising the resurrected Jesus. Praise Him even in the midst of any doubts or difficulties you have. Ask Him to show you Himself as the way, the truth, and the life (see John 14:6).

DAY 3

CREED

The power that united the apostles, launched the first church, and invaded the Roman Empire was the certain knowledge and belief that Jesus had physically risen from the dead:

> With great power the apostles continued to testify
> to the resurrection of the Lord Jesus. And God's
> grace was … powerfully at work in them all.
> **ACTS 4:33, NIV**

In Romans 1:4 Paul proclaimed that Jesus "was declared the Son of God with power by the resurrection from the dead" (NASB). Paul's personal testimony and message were that through the resurrection, Jesus demonstrated that He is utterly unique. Jesus Christ has the power not only to lay down his life but also to take it up again (see John 10:18).

Without the resurrection there would be no good news, and the New Testament would not even make sense.

If you had a meter that could measure the power of the testimony of today's church about the resurrection, what would it read? Place a mark on the scale.

1	2	3	4	5
PATHETIC				POWERFUL

Why did you choose this power rating, and what can the church do to improve it?

The resurrection narratives are found in all four Gospels and the Book of Acts (see Matt. 27:62–28:20; Mark 16; Luke 24; John 20–21; Acts 1:1-12). Therefore, if you ask Christians where to find the best evidence for Jesus' resurrection, most normally point to the Gospels. The Gospel writers are excellent sources, but they are not the earliest sources for the resurrection of Jesus.

The apostle Paul is our best and earliest source for understanding when Christians came to believe in the bodily resurrection of Jesus. Paul also detailed reasons we can have hope for our own limitless resurrection bodies. In 1 Corinthians 15 Paul passed on the most important and earliest Christian creed:

> I delivered to you as of first importance what I also received: that Christ died for our sins in accordance with the Scriptures, that he was buried, that he was raised on the third day in accordance with the Scriptures, and that he appeared to Cephas, then to the twelve. Then he appeared to more than five hundred brothers at one time, most of whom are still alive, though some have fallen asleep. Then he appeared to James, then to all the apostles.
>
> **1 CORINTHIANS 15:3-7, ESV**

A creed is a formal statement of Christian beliefs.[5] In the Old Testament the Shema (see Deut. 6:4-9) would be characterized as a creedal statement.

What creeds (more broadly defined, perhaps a mission statement or set of values) does your church or small group have?

■ JESUS' POSTRESURRECTION APPEARANCES

- Women leaving the tomb area (Matt. 28:9-10)
- Mary Magdalene (Mark 16:9-10; John 20:14-17)
- 2 disciples on the road to Emmaus (Mark 16:12-13; Luke 24:13-31)
- Peter (Luke 24:34; 1 Cor. 15:5)
- 10 disciples in the upper room (Luke 24:36-49; John 20:19-23)
- 11 disciples in the upper room (Mark 16:14; John 20:26-31; 1 Cor. 15:5)
- 7 disciples fishing (John 21:1-23)
- The disciples on a Galilee mountain (Matt. 28:16-20; Mark 16:15-18)
- More than 500 (1 Cor. 15:6)
- James and then all the apostles (1 Cor. 15:7)
- The ascension (Mark 16:19; Luke 24:50-51; Acts 1:7-9)
- Paul (Acts 9:3-6)[6]

List evidence for the resurrection in 1 Corinthians 15:3-7.

The source material for this creed is the oldest in the New Testament. It stretches back to within weeks of the resurrection event itself. The scholar James Dunn is "entirely confident" in stating that the tradition behind the composition of 1 Corinthians 15:3-4 "formulated … within months of Jesus' death."[7] Gary Habermas has compiled a comprehensive citation of biblical scholars, from across the theological spectrum, who agree on the early development of this central tradition.[8]

Why do you think the Corinthians needed to be reminded of basic facts about the gospel?

Paul passed on this early Christian creed (1 Cor. 15:3-7) to the Corinthian church in A.D. 53–55. This is the earliest declaration of faith in oral circulation before it was ever committed to writing. These early creeds preserved the Christian faith before the New Testament was written. Keep in mind that the very first Christian generation did not have a Bible as we know it today. Therefore, these early creeds and hyms were extremely important in teaching the basics of the faith.

Paul didn't invent this creed. How do we know that? He said, "I delivered to you … what I also received" (v. 3, NASB). Earlier in his letter Paul used the same formulaic language, "I received from the Lord what I also delivered to you" (1 Cor. 11:23, ESV), in describing how the church should conduct the Lord's Supper. Paul was passing on a tradition that predates his letter to the Corinthian church—what early Christians came to believe about the resurrection and also when they believed it. It is plausible, if not probable, that this most important Christian creed began in the earliest Christian worship services as prayers, songs, or preaching exhortations.

Another resurrection tradition unique to early Christian texts was a new day of communal worship. The day of worship for Christians migrated from the Jewish Sabbath to Sunday, resurrection day ("the third day"), as a continuing testimony to the centrality of the resurrection (see Acts 20:7). For Christians, resurrection is not celebrated on Easter alone but every Lord's Day. The phrase "the first day of the week" was not found in Jewish tradition until the Gospel writers.[9]

Think about how important the gathering of the local church was to the first Christians. Should it not be the same with us today? Every time we gather on the first day of the week, we give a testimony about Jesus' resurrection.

End today's study by thanking God for your church and small group. Then pray in affirmation to the triune God, using the following as prayer starters.

Father, I believe that You …

Jesus, You are my …

Holy Spirit, I thank You for …

DAY 4

THE ARABIA EXPERIENCE

The apostle Paul came to believe in the gospel of Jesus through the miraculous Damascus Road experience. This came after Jesus' resurrection. He went from persecuting and killing Christians to loving Jesus because of the resurrection. Have you ever stopped to consider that Paul, unlike the other apostles, met Jesus after the resurrection? Jesus' disciples all met Jesus prior to His passion and resurrection; Paul knew Jesus as the Resurrection—the same way we know Jesus today.

How did Paul come to this unshakable, unquenchable belief in Jesus and the resurrection? When did he receive this this creed, this resurrection material that he passed on to the church of Corinth (see 1 Cor. 15:3-7)? And what difference does it make to our lives today? Those are the questions we will seek to answer today.

The villainous and psychotic Emperor Nero (who reigned A.D. 54–68) martyred the apostle Paul around A.D. 65 (Peter was also most likely martyred by Nero in A.D. 65). Nero's persecution of Christians began in A.D. 64. This is an important fact because Paul would have obviously completed all of his epistles prior to his martyrdom.

Paul was converted to Christianity about two years after the crucifixion and resurrection of Jesus. According to Galatians 1:18, Paul visited Jerusalem three years after his conversion on the road to Damascus. What was Paul doing for those three years? In verse 17 Paul said he went first to Arabia and then to Damascus to spend time with God, most possibly in prayer, study, and meditation. He decided to go to God first rather than "consult any human being" (v. 16, NIV), even the other apostles.

Take a moment to put yourself in Paul's shoes at this point in his life. Can you imagine how Paul felt? He had overseen Stephen's martyrdom and had systematically persecuted Christians. Then he met the resurrected Jesus.

Identify what kinds of emotions you would have had if you were Paul.

So Paul ran to Arabia. For three years he wrestled with God, and like Jacob before him, who wrestled with God and was left with a limp (see Gen. 32:22-32), God left Paul with a thorn in the flesh to keep him dependent on Him. Paul was alone with God for three years.

N. T. Wright has pointed out some unique parallels between Paul's Arabia experience and Elijah's retreat to Horeb to escape Jezebel.[10] Just as Elijah went into the wilderness to die but was spiritually resurrected (see 1 Kings 19), Paul had a spiritual resurrection in Arabia. Like Elijah, Paul left Arabia and went into Damascus, where God, ahead of Paul, had instructed a Christian man named Ananias to care for him.

Perhaps, like Paul, you think you have done the unimaginable. Maybe you have regret for past actions or feel that you have failed. Many Christ followers still feel that God could never use them. And yet consider the flawed people in the Bible whom God used. The key point is that ironically, Paul, the earliest written witness of the resurrection of Jesus, once killed Christians. God can use anyone who yields to Him.

Do you need an Arabia experience with God, a time to spend alone with Him and seek His healing, direction, and purpose? Describe what this would look like for you.

Spend time with God as you end today's study. Seek His wisdom and insight into any questions you have, decisions you need to make, or direction in life you are seeking. Then read John 11:25-26 and answer the question Jesus posed to Martha:

> I am the resurrection and the life. The one who believes
> in me will live, even though they die; and whoever lives
> by believing in me will never die. Do you believe this?
> **JOHN 11:25-26, NIV**

Record the way you would honestly respond to Jesus, using one of the following prompts.

Yes, Lord, I believe that You are the resurrection and the life and that I will live because …

I am still struggling with the resurrection because …

RESURRECTION BODIES

As followers of Jesus, we live by faith in the tension between two resurrections: Jesus' first resurrection and our own. The bodily resurrection of Jesus guarantees our future bodily resurrection. They are linked:

> Christ has indeed been raised from the dead,
> the firstfruits of those who have fallen asleep.
> **1 CORINTHIANS 15:20, NIV**

> Our citizenship is in heaven. And we eagerly await
> a Savior from there, the Lord Jesus Christ, who, by
> the power that enables Him to bring everything
> under His control, will transform our lowly bodies
> so that they will be like his glorious body.
>
> **PHILIPPIANS 3:20-21, NIV**

What do these two passages teach you about your connection to Jesus in relation to your own eventual resurrection?

Thanks to the resurrection of Jesus, Christians are promised that the best is yet to come and that death is only the beginning, not the end. That is why the apostle Paul told the Thessalonian Christians who had lost their loved ones that though we grieve, we do not grieve like those who have no hope, because we know it is only a short interlude until we see them again (see 1 Thess. 4:13).

The promise of 1 Corinthians 15 is that our deceased loved ones have not died in vain (see vv. 16-18). But there is more. In the same passage Paul answered at least three vital questions that give us hope now and in the future.

1. WHAT WILL THE RESURRECTION BE LIKE?

Read 1 Corinthians 15:51-52.

Cosmic signs and miracles will hasten the resurrection of the dead. The dead will rise suddenly. Loud noises will accompany this apocalyptic hastening of the dead. In Thessalonians Paul stated that three different sounds will be heard at the resurrection: the cry or command of the Lord Himself, the voice of an archangel, and the trumpet of God (see 1 Thess. 4:16).

2. WHAT KIND OF RESURRECTION BODY CAN WE EXPECT?

Read 1 Corinthians 15:35-44,50-56.

Our resurrection body will be a literal, physical body, not a spirit-ghost or apparition. We know this because Paul tells the church at Philippi that Christ will "transform our lowly body to be like his glorious body" (Phil. 3:21). Christ was raised in a physical body and Scripture tells us that our resurrection bodies will be patterned after His own body. Jesus also tells His disciples:

> See my hands and my feet, that it is I myself.
> Touch me, and see. For a spirit does not have
> flesh and bones as you see that I have.
> **LUKE 24:39, ESV**

A belief in the resurrection also drove Christians to value all life, which included caring for the body in burial. It is not surprising that Christians desired to be buried together; however, they innovated new terminology for their burial practices, *cemetery (koimeterion)*, or *sleeping place*, because death was peacefully thought of as rest or sleep, a temporary holding place.[11]

This early Christian burial terminology had an inherent resurrection perspective, in contrast to the wider Roman terminology for burial—*mausoleum* for the wealthy or *sepulchre* for placing ashes. Body dumping was a significant problem in Rome. It has been estimated that at least 1,500 corpses were abandoned annually.[12] Corpses of the destitute, slaves, and poor were thrown into mass pits, forgotten to eternity.[13] The fact that early Christians cared for each individual body in burial because of a resurrection-centric faith is one reason for the rapid spread of the movement among the poor and slave classes in the Roman Empire.

Paul used two descriptive words to characterize resurrection life in verse 53 (NIV): *imperishable* (a body that never needs to be upgraded) and *immortality* (a body that will never die). Paul's clear description of the resurrected state underscores why he stated his desire to be with Jesus: "To me, to live is Christ and to die is gain" (Phil. 1:21, NIV).

The author of Revelation, quoting the words of the resurrected Jesus, made it clear that Jesus' resurrected body will never die again:

> I am the Living One; I was dead, and
> now look, I am alive for ever and ever!
> **REVELATION 1:18, NIV**

Luke's Gospel records Jesus' description of the resurrection from the dead. He explicitly stated those who are resurrected "can no longer die" (Luke 20:36, NIV).

It is difficult to watch our bodies break down. Are you feeling a little sore today? Is your body weaker than it once was? Are you having more "senior moments"? Are you fighting a disease?

Our resurrection bodies will be "raised in glory; ... raised in power" (1 Cor. 15:43, NIV). As believers, we know death is not the end. That doesn't mean we look forward to death, but as Pastor Greg Laurie tweeted, "Only those who are prepared to die are really ready to live."[14]

3. WHY DOES THE RESURRECTION MATTER FOR US TODAY? HOW SHOULD WE LIVE OUR LIVES NOW?

Read 1 Corinthians 15:30-34,57-58.

If the resurrection never happened, Paul said, the early Christians may as well stop suffering for Christ and dedicate their lives to pleasure (see 1 Cor 15:30-32). However, because Jesus has been raised, Paul stated that Christians should pursue holy living (see vv. 33-34). From the beginning Christianity has taught that the resurrection was not something to be embarrassed about but something to proclaim and, if necessary, to sacrifice our lives for.

> What are some of the biggest differences between the way someone who believes in the resurrection and someone who does not believe should live their lives?

Paul concluded this teaching with a powerful point in verse 58. What happens in the future with your resurrection body affects everything you do for God today. That is why Paul used the present tense, "Your labor in the Lord is not in vain" (NIV), rather than the future tense, "Your labor will not be in vain." He was challenging believers never to give up, never to quit, but to "be steadfast, immovable, always excelling in the Lord's work" (HCSB). The resurrection not only shapes our future but also energizes our present ministry for the kingdom of God.

We should never lack motivation to serve God with all our heart, because we know everything we do for God will last for all eternity. Any suffering we endure for Jesus' sake will be worth it when we see Him and are welcomed into His eternal kingdom.

Christians can be as solid as a rock—steadfast and immovable—because since the worst enemy, death, is defeated, we have nothing to fear. We need to be strong. The resurrection promises us that our lives have eternal significance when devoted to our ever-living, resurrected Lord.

If you knew with certainty that you would live forever, what would you do differently? What risks would you take?

Read engagement principle 1 in the box. Is it difficult or easy for you to listen attentively to someone who has doubts about Jesus and the truth of Scripture? Why?

Close your study time in prayer, praising God for the resurrection. Thank Him that your life on earth and the deaths of your loved ones are not in vain. Finish your prayer as many in the early church did: "Come, Lord Jesus!"

■ ENGAGEMENT PRINCIPLE 1

SHUT UP AND LISTEN

To guide someone to the truth, you must be a great listener. Start with where people are, not by immediately quoting Scripture. Remember, your goal is not to win a debate at all costs but to build the foundation of a trusting relationship through which you can show compassion and share biblical truth when the person is ready to hear it.

Instead of dominating the conversation, start where this person is. Listen attentively to what they have to say and what they believe. What do they believe about Jesus? What biases are evident? Why do they believe as they do? What spiritual needs do you detect? Your posture is open and inviting. Because you are inquisitive about what this person has to say, ask follow-up questions and give nonverbal and verbal clues that you hear what they are saying. Put the person's need to know Jesus above yourself and your need to win an argument.

PARANORMAL: THE NEW NORMAL

HOW SHOULD CHRISTIANS RESPOND TO SPIRITUAL DARKNESS AND PARANORMAL ACTIVITY?

START

C. S. Lewis became a celebrity in North America with the release of his wartime best seller *The Screwtape Letters*. It originally appeared as a series of articles published in a church magazine. The letters were popular enough that a year later they were imported into a small book for a wider popular audience. *The Screwtape Letters* challenged the mind and stretched the heart. In the preface Lewis identified two wrong attitudes toward the Devil, attitudes that are perhaps even more prevalent today:

> There are two equal and opposite errors into which our race can fall about the devils. One is to disbelieve in their existence. The other is to believe, and to feel an excessive and unhealthy interest in them.[1]

What are the dangers of both of these errors?

As you contemplate Lewis's point, how would you evaluate your perception of and attitude toward spiritual darkness?

In what areas of our culture do you see evidence of increasing interest in the paranormal?

The purpose of this session is to make us aware of how demons work in our lives and in the world so that we can avoid giving them a foothold. Let's watch and listen to what Jeremiah has to say about this important topic.

WATCH

1. The paranormal is attractive and has become normal in our society.

2. The paranormal teaches a false gospel, makes promises it cannot keep, and will always bring me into bondage and confusion.

3. Only Jesus Christ can set me free. Only in Jesus can I know the purpose for my life. Only in Jesus can I experience lasting peace. And only in Jesus can I truly know the truth.

RESPOND

What one truth from Jeremiah's teaching resonated most with you?

Read Ephesians 6:10-20.

What did Paul assume about the Devil (Satan) and the demonic world?

As a group, list each piece of the armor and how it protects and arms believers for spiritual warfare.

Unfortunately, many Christians are not aware of their identity and authority in Jesus Christ. Unprepared believers lack confidence not only to discuss the Devil and demons but also to overcome them. A Christian's power and confidence to overcome the devil do not occur automatically. Notice the action words Paul used in Ephesians 6: "Put on the full armor of God" (v. 11, NASB). "Take up the full armor of God" (v. 13, NASB). "Stand firm therefore, having girded your loins with truth" (v. 14, NASB). " [Take] up the shield of faith" (v. 16, NASB). "Take the helmet of salvation" (v. 17, NASB). These action words describe a believer's continual work to overcome the Enemy when he strikes, and strike he will. Paul taught that we are active agents, not passive observers, in battling demonic forces.

Read 2 Corinthians 2:11.

Paul wrote about Satan to the Corinthian church more than he did to any of the other churches. Paul must have recognized demonic attack in the church and tried to warn them. Scripture refers to Satan as the deceiver (see 2 John 7) and the father of lies (see John 8:44). Here Paul warned the church not to let Satan outwit them, because he is also a schemer.

> **What are some ways Satan can outwit us?**

> **When have you experienced or witnessed Satan's schemes? What did you learn about his tactics? About spiritual warfare? About yourself?**

In battle we need fellow allies in the foxhole with us—companions who will fight with us and for us. Our small group is like a platoon; we are comrades in this spiritual battle.

> **How can we support one another in the fight against the Devil's schemes?**

In this week's personal study we will investigate what the Bible says about demons and the battleground of the mind.

PRAY

Prayer is indispensable in spiritual warfare. An important part of our group commitment as a platoon of fellow warriors is to pray with and for one another.

- Pray that you will be more aware of Satan's schemes in your daily lives.
- Ask God to give each of you His power to stand against the Devil's schemes.
- Pray for the specific needs of group members, especially anyone who needs God's strength for spiritual battle.
- Pray for opportunities to get out of your comfort zones and be ambassadors for Christ.

Read week 3 and complete the activities on the following pages before the next group experience.

DAY 1

AN EPIC BATTLE

The core of Jesus' mission was preaching the establishment of the kingdom of God. Indeed, the kingdom of God was inseparably linked to the gospel or good news, for which Israel and the world had waited. But a striking yet, more often than not, overlooked feature in Jesus' preaching was His linking of the kingdom of God with exorcism. Exorcism was not a sidebar issue in Jesus' ministry. Exorcism was emblematic and in fact gave evidence of the destruction of Satan and the power of Jesus.

Exorcisms continued after Jesus, even throughout Paul's ministry.

Read Acts 19:11-20.

We have a culture that is obsessed with the paranormal. Paranormal entertainment, psychic fairs, ghost stories and countless other expressions of paranormal involvement have commanded our bookstores and TV, computer, and movie screens. Just as the paranormal is popular in our world, exorcism was big business in the first century. You could make a fine living as a professional exorcist in late antiquity. Unfortunately, in Acts 19 we see firsthand what happens when you meet a demon unprepared.

It is important to notice that the text states these Jewish exorcists were traveling professionals "who went from place to place" (v. 13, NASB). Luke offered an interesting layer of detail, noting that the humiliated professional exorcists were overpowered and left the demonic encounter naked. Similar to the uniforms worn today by professional sports teams, exorcists in the first century were adorned with special clothing that would enhance their powers against the dark world. The fame and power of Jesus' name had evidently spread so much that Jewish exorcists were happy to use the name of Jesus (the implication is that these Jews were using the name of Jesus professionally but had no allegiance to Jesus personally). It did not matter that the Jewish exorcists were armored like ancient ghost busters or wizards; they were unprepared and utterly defeated.

In contrast, Jesus' power was such that He defeated demons with a single word:

> That evening they brought to him many who were
> oppressed by demons, and he cast out the spirits
> with a word and healed all who were sick.
> **MATTHEW 8:16, ESV**

Jesus appointed twelve apostles "to preach and have authority to cast out demons" (Mark 3:14-15, ESV). Luke emphasized the linkage between proclaiming the gospel of the kingdom of God and exorcism:

> He called the twelve together and gave them power
> and authority over all demons and to cure diseases,
> and he sent them out to proclaim the kingdom of God
> and to heal. And they departed and went through the
> villages, preaching the gospel and healing everywhere.
> **LUKE 9:1-2,6, ESV**

■ THE DARK WORLD OF THE OCCULT

The word *occult*, meaning *hidden*, refers to supernatural influences, agencies, or phenomena. Here are three modern occult practices and a brief biblical response to each.

1. OCCULT DIVINATION claims to predict the future. The term divination refers to methods of obtaining knowledge of the unknown or the future by means of omens. Probably, the most popular form of divination is astrology, which claims that heavenly bodies exert an influence on people.

Astrology is incompatible with biblical teachings. God is the Creator of everything, including the stars, moon, and planets (see Gen. 1:14-18). These bodies are created objects, not gods. Astrology attempts to predict the future (see Matt. 24:36), but Jesus said we have no reason to be anxious about tomorrow (see Matt. 6:25,34). We are to place faith in God for the future and to consult the Bible for the guidance we need for living. The Bible condemns astrology as a pagan religious practice (see Deut. 4:19; Isa. 2:6; 47:12-14).

2. SPIRITUALISM seeks to communicate with the dead. Spiritualism is the belief that spirits of the dead communicate with the living. The heart of spiritualism is the seance, through which the spirit world is allegedly contacted by a medium.

The Bible clearly condemns spiritualism. Spiritualist practices are detestable aspects of pagan practices and inevitably defile the authentic worship of God (see Lev. 20:6; 2 Kings 23; Isa. 19:3). Believers are warned not to tolerate mediums and spiritualists. God condemned Saul for consulting a witch (medium; see 1 Chron. 10:13-14). God speaks of the foolishness of consulting mediums and the dead when we serve a living God (see Isa. 8:19).

3. SATANISM glorifies evil. Satanists worship Satan as their lord and live their lives openly opposed to Christianity. Some Satanists insist that they do not believe in a literal Satan but consider him a symbol of evil and their lifestyle. In any case, the end result of Satanism is the destruction of the individual and/or someone else. All Satanists have in common their love of evil and their opposition to Christ and His kingdom. The lord who has control of their lives is none other than Satan Himself, the archenemy of God.

Believers must remember that Satan is not equal with God. He is a created being whom Jesus has already defeated on the cross. Christians can resist Satan by claiming Christ's victory (see 1 John 3:8; Col. 2:15), by resisting temptation (see 1 Cor. 10:13; Jas. 4:7), and by walking daily in the power of God's Holy Spirit (see 1 John 4:4). We also have spiritual weapons that God provides to fight the Devil (see Eph. 6:11-18).[2]

Is it easier to participate in the paranormal in our culture today or to ignore it all together? Why are both of these actions dangerous?

Besides giving the disciples the power and authority over demons and diseases, what did Jesus send the disciples out to do? How can this be applied to Jesus' followers today?

Spend time praying that God will make you aware of the reality of the paranormal around you. Ask that He will equip you to proclaim the kingdom of God in a world where the Devil is spreading the lie that being involved with this dark world is innocent.

DAY 2

THE KINGDOM OF GOD VS. THE KINGDOM OF SATAN

It is an often-repeated Christian cliché that the Christian life is not a playground; it is a battleground. The problem with this statement is that most followers of Jesus are not ready for battle with this "dark world" (Eph. 6:12, NIV). Fighting against the forces of darkness sounds good in a Bible setting, but it is difficult to live out. We now turn to the origins and activity of demons.

We learn more about the Devil and demons from the four Gospels than any other biblical books. Demons can cause illness (see Matt. 10:1; 17:15-18), agony (see 15:22), loss of the ability to speak (see 9:32), and pain (see 17:15). *Demon*, which is translated from the Greek *daimon*, is not the exclusive name for Satan's minions. Because there is no Hebrew word for *demon*, the Gospels frequently use the Old Testament language of *unclean* or *evil spirit*. For example, King Saul was tormented several times by an "evil spirit" (1 Sam. 16:14-15; 18:10; 19:9).

It is noteworthy that the plural *demons* is used 63 times in the New Testament (53 of which are in the Gospels), far more than the singular *demon*. The popular modern term *demon-possessed* or *demon possession* does not occur in the Greek New Testament. In the original New Testament we never read of a demon possessing another person. The proper terminology for "having a demon" or "being controlled by a demon" is "to be demonized." Merrill Unger described the abilities of demons this way: "As spiritual beings, demons are intelligent, vicious, unclean, with power to afflict men with physical hurt, and moral and spiritual contamination."[3]

While some of these definitions may seem extreme or even bizarre, we must remember that the New Testament writers continually affirmed both that demons exist and that they are active in the world.

Read the following passages.

You believe that there is one God. You do well.
Even the demons believe—and tremble!
JAMES 2:19, NKJV

As he was still coming, the demon threw him down and
convulsed him. Then Jesus rebuked the unclean spirit,
healed the child, and gave him back to his father.
LUKE 9:42, NKJV

He will also say to those on the left hand, "Depart
from Me, you cursed, into the everlasting fire
prepared for the devil and his angels."
MATTHEW 25:41, NKJV

If someone asked you to explain why you believe demons exist, what would you say?

Demons are fallen angels who joined Satan in his rebellion against God. The timing of this event is impossible to date, but some Bible commentators place the rebellion between verses 1 and 2 of Genesis 1. The apostle Peter wrote:

God did not spare angels when they sinned, but sent them to
hell, putting them in chains of darkness to be held for judgment.
2 PETER 2:4, NIV

We know that the reason these former angels were cast out of heaven was
because of their sin. Jude recorded:

The angels who did not keep their positions of
authority but abandoned their proper dwelling—
these he has kept in darkness, bound with everlasting
chains for judgment on the great Day.
JUDE 6, NIV

Many Bible interpreters believe that Ezekiel 28:11-19, as well as Isaiah 14:12-15,
describes the fall of Satan. If it does, this passage provides interesting facts
about Satan and his fall.

Read Ezekiel 28:11-19.

What facts do you learn about Satan and demons in this passage?

We have become accustomed to power rankings in sports. Did you know the
Devil has power rankings too? Satan's enterprise is organized and regimented.
It is a satanic axis of evil with at least four specific layers. Paul mentioned these
in Ephesians 6:12:

We do not wrestle against flesh and blood, but
against the rulers, against the authorities, against the
cosmic powers over this present darkness, against
the spiritual forces of evil in the heavenly places.
EPHESIANS 6:12, ESV

Let's look at these four levels in detail.

LEVEL 1: RULERS AND PRINCIPALITIES. Demons work to influence world
leaders and all who are in authority. They are known as principalities:

> The prince of the kingdom of Persia withstood
> me twenty-one days; and behold, Michael, one
> of the chief princes, came to help me, for I had
> been left alone there with the kings of Persia.
> **DANIEL 10:13, NKJV**

> Do you know why I have come to you? And now I must
> return to fight with the prince of Persia; and when I have
> gone forth, indeed the prince of Greece will come.
> **DANIEL 10:20, NKJV**

This unique conversation gives us a glimpse into the unseen realm of angelic warfare. Daniel's faithful prayer was heard, but the answer was not immediate because of demonic intervention. In fact, the prince of Persia (a territorial spirit demonically influencing the rulers of Persia to combat the plan of Almighty God) overpowered the angelic messenger sent with the answer to Daniel's prayer. Daniel received the answer to his prayers only when the archangel Michael joined the righteous angel to oppose this territorial demonic influence. From this passage we understand the responsibilities we have as believers to pray for our leaders regularly and fervently. Paul echoed this idea in the New Testament:

> I exhort first of all that supplications, prayers, intercessions,
> and giving of thanks be made for all men, for kings
> and all who are in authority, that we may lead a quiet
> and peaceable life in all godliness and reverence.
> **1 TIMOTHY 2:1-2, NKJV**

If God has placed you in a position of leadership and authority, Satan's special agents are targeting you. Stay humble, stay on your knees, and seek God, for your weapons are mighty through Him (see 2 Cor. 10:3-5).

Take a moment to record a prayer for government officials: the president, Congress, judges, and officials at the state and local levels.

LEVEL 2: AUTHORITIES. Paul most frequently mentioned the first two tiers of demons: rulers and authorities (see Eph. 1:21; 3:10). In Ephesians 2 Paul referred to this demonic hierarchy:

> You were dead in the trespasses and sins in which
> you once walked, following the course of this world,
> following the prince of the power of the air, the spirit
> that is now at work in the sons of disobedience.
> **EPHESIANS 2:1-2, ESV**

LEVEL 3: COSMIC POWERS OVER THIS PRESENT AGE. Paul was writing to the Ephesian church. Ephesus was the home of the temple of Diana/Artemis, a Greek goddess, and the temple was one of the seven ancient wonders of the world. We can speculate that Paul intended all false gods when he referred to "rulers of the darkness of this age" (Eph. 6:12, NKJV), who poison the hearts and minds of people made in God's image.[4] In 1 Corinthians Paul spoke of the demonic influence of the pagan gods and the unwitting intersection of paganism and demonism:

> What pagans sacrifice they offer to demons and not to
> God. I do not want you to be participants with demons.
> **1 CORINTHIANS 10:20, ESV**

What are the false gods people look to in today's world? How do they poison the hearts and minds of people made in God's image?

LEVEL 4: SPIRITUAL FORCES OF EVIL IN THE HEAVENLY PLACES. This is a catch-all phrase for evil spirits of all ranks. Paul is not interested in every aspect of the demonic organizational chart; rather, he wants believers in Christ to know the power and organization of the Enemy so that "we are not ignorant of his designs" (2 Cor. 2:11, ESV). The Devil constantly deploys his emissaries against believers through various methods: temptation (see 1 Thess. 3:5), evil thoughts and desires (see Acts 5:3), attempts to attack believers (see 1 Pet. 5:8), corruption and confusion of the mind (see 2 Cor. 11:3), and doubt (see Gen. 3:1).

Is it surprising that demons under Satan's dominion are so well organized? What does this fact indicate to you about them?

How can an increased awareness of demons' characteristics and functions help you navigate your life as a Christ follower?

As you close your study today, pray, asking God for His wisdom and strength as you live in a world of unseen spiritual warfare. Continue to pray for government officials, as well as anyone under the influence of demonic powers.

DAY 3

GOD'S POWERFUL RESOURCES FOR BELIEVERS

Spiritual warfare is not your battle; it is God's battle. Therefore, God has supplied you with all the necessary armor and machinery to lay siege to your spiritual enemies and be victorious:

> Though we walk in the flesh, we do not war according to the flesh. For the weapons of our warfare are not carnal but mighty in God for pulling down strongholds, casting down arguments and every high thing that exalts itself against the knowledge of God, bringing every thought into captivity to the obedience of Christ.
> **2 CORINTHIANS 10:3-5, NKJV**

Paul regularly used militaristic language to describe spiritual conflict, perseverance, and vibrant faith in the Christian life. Paul stated that we do not "war according to the flesh" (2 Cor. 10:3, NKJV), which in the Greek is *strateuo*, from which we transliterate the English word *strategy*. Spiritual victory includes God-given spiritual tactics to overcome the Enemy. It is not a human or fleshly method. The follower of Jesus can overcome the strength of the paranormal world only by applying God's strategy for victory with the strength and weapons God provides.

Paul continued:

> The weapons of our warfare are not of the flesh
> but have divine power to destroy strongholds.
> **2 CORINTHIANS 10:4, ESV**

In this verse Paul alluded to the wisdom of Proverbs in describing spiritual weapons:

> A wise man scales the city of the mighty
> and brings down the stronghold in which they trust.
> **PROVERBS 21:22, ESV**

Through the indwelling presence of the Holy Spirit, believers have access to destructive weapons designed to obliterate the Devil's schemes to entrap and enslave. It is in Christ that we destroy the works of the Devil.

In the next verse Paul emphasized:

> We destroy arguments and every lofty opinion
> raised against the knowledge of God.
> **2 CORINTHIANS 10:5, ESV**

In Christ we storm the walls of the Enemy and lay siege through our mighty weapons in God. Paul used the military term *destroy* to depict the complete annihilation of the Devil's strongholds by our spiritually energized battering rams, catapults, and mobile-assault towers.

What strongholds need to be destroyed in your life? What strongholds need to be demolished in your family?

What thoughts need to be taken hostage to the truth of God's Word?

In our group discussion we highlighted the action words Paul employed to describe believers' preparation to be victorious in spiritual warfare. Reread Ephesians 6:10-20 and complete the following activities as you close your time today.

How prepared are you for spiritual warfare? What specific steps are you taking to increase your preparedness?

How would the weapons Paul mentioned help you battle the strongholds you have identified?

Notice the role of prayer in verse 18. Write a prayer for God to strengthen you with His mighty weapons to break the chains in your life.

■ HOW TO DEMOLISH SPIRITUAL STRONGHOLDS

A spiritual stronghold is an idea, a thought process, a habit, or an addiction through which Satan has influence in your life. Use this biblical process to break free.

1. IDENTIFY the stronghold and the reason it violates God's Word and God's will.

2. REPENT of the sin and ask for God's forgiveness.

3. DECLARE WAR on the stronghold by substituting biblical truth, claiming the mind of Christ, using spiritual weapons (see Eph. 6:13-17), praying for the Holy Spirit's power and guidance, requesting others' prayers and support, boldly making God's truth clear, and claiming the victory by faith.

4. PRAY as you put on each piece of spiritual armor (see Eph. 6:13-17) and receive God's strength to fight the obstacle.

5. WIN the victory in Christ by loving God, keeping His commandments, being sure you are born of God, believing Jesus is God's Son, and believing God keeps you safe (see 1 John 4:4; 5:2-3,18-20).[5]

DAY 4

THE DEMONS' DOOM

In the first three days of this week's study, you learned what the Bible says demons are and what their mission is in the world. But they won't always have free rein in the world. What will become of them?

Recalling what you have learned about demons, how do you feel about them?

- ☐ Fear
- ☐ Ambivalence
- ☐ Trust in God
- ☐ Nothing; I'm not sure they really exist.
- ☐ Other:

Why?

Scripture assures us that demonic activity will increase as we approach Christ's second coming. We see the evidence in the world today with massive tragedies, shootings, and terrorist attacks. Paul informs us:

> Evil men and impostors will grow worse
> and worse, deceiving and being deceived.
> **2 TIMOTHY 3:13, NKJV**

What signs of the end times are you noticing? Are evil and deception in the world getting worse? If so, in what ways do you see them?

Notice the context of 2 Timothy 3:13. It comes in the middle of Paul's charge to his son in the faith, Timothy, about living a godly life in an evil world. This is vital. In the last days, as evil and deception become more and more commonplace, Christ followers must rely even more on God's Word. It is the only way to tell the true from the false.

Unknowingly, many people who are not followers of Jesus are under the control and influence of demons. Though not popular to admit in a sophisticated society such as the United States, it is certainly true that the Enemy is at work, albeit covertly. Second Corinthians 11:14 says, "Satan disguises himself as an angel of light" (ESV). At other times we observe darkness personified more overtly, for example, in a mass shooting at a movie theater, where innocent people are murdered. During those times we are reminded that Satan is lurking behind the scenes influencing and destroying lives.

Read Ephesians 2:1-3.

This passage is talking about the way we used to live before we began following Jesus Christ. The spirit of Satan is at work in those who are disobedient.

> **What does this passage reveal to you about Satan's connection with the world?**

Read 1 John 4:1-3.

> **How can you "test the spirits" (v. 1, ESV) so that you are not influenced by false teaching or other evil?**

Given the reality and prevalence of satanic activity in the world, we can find encouragement by learning about the destruction of the Devil and all the demonic forces:

> The angels who did not stay within their own
> position of authority, but left their proper dwelling,
> he has kept in eternal chains under gloomy
> darkness until the judgment of the great day.
> **JUDE 6, ESV**

> He will say to those on his left, "Depart from me, you cursed,
> into the eternal fire prepared for the devil and his angels."
> **MATTHEW 25:41, ESV**

The clear teaching of the New Testament is that a judgment day is coming for Satan. From the lips of Jesus we learn that hell was created for the Devil, and a day is appointed for him to be cast into eternal fire and punishment.

Perhaps this is one reason the demons tremble at the presence of God (see Jas. 2:19). In Matthew 8:29 demons exclaimed in the presence of Jesus:

> What have we to do with You, Jesus, You Son of God?
> Have You come here to torment us before the time?
> **MATTHEW 8:29, NKJV**

It seems that demons are acutely aware of their defeat. In fact, they are already defeated. Jesus' triumph on the cross was not only to rescue humankind from sin but also to vanquish the Enemy of God:

> Now is the time for judgment on this world;
> now the prince of this world will be driven out.
> **JOHN 12:31, NIV**

Jesus came to destroy Satan's works and, ultimately, Satan and his demons themselves. Although Satan is still the ruler of this world (see John 14:30; 1 John 5:19), he is already defeated because of Jesus' sacrifice. The apostle John described the eventual fate of Satan (and his demons with him):

> The devil, who deceived them, was thrown into
> the lake of burning sulfur, where the beast and
> the false prophet had been thrown. They will be
> tormented day and night for ever and ever.
> **REVELATION 20:10, NIV**

Want some good news? Satan's reign, control, and power will not last forever. He is a created being, a fallen angel; he is not eternal. He has been manipulating, deceiving, lying, murdering, and creating evil and chaos since he deceived our earliest ancestors. But his doom is sealed.

How does this understanding of the ultimate future of Satan and his demons encourage you?

We've surveyed the future destruction of the Devil and his demonic cohort, but what about your future? Do you know Christ personally? If not, now is the perfect time for you to make certain that your sins are forgiven and that you have peace with God through Jesus Christ. Are you in Christ? Have you trusted the Lord Jesus Christ for the forgiveness of your sins and eternal life in heaven? If you have not, I pray that today will be your day of decision. There is not a specific prayer or formulaic statement that will begin your eternal relationship with God. It is a matter of trust. The Bible says in John 1:12:

> To all who did receive him, who believed in his name,
> he gave the right to become children of God.
> **JOHN 1:12, ESV**

You can express your trust in Christ by saying a prayer, although it is not the words that redeem you. Say this prayer to God:

> Lord Jesus, I admit that I am sinner who cannot save myself. I place my trust in You, the resurrected Christ, for the forgiveness of my sins and eternal life in heaven. Today I begin my eternal relationship with You. Help me now to live for You.

If you are indeed in Christ—you believe in Him and you are following Him as your Savior and the Lord of your life—take a moment now and thank Him for what He has done to make His saving grace available to you. Also thank Him for His protection of you from evil. Take a moment to pray for at least one friend, group member, coworker, or neighbor who is not yet in Christ. Ask God to reveal Himself to them and to draw them to Himself.

If you are not yet in Christ, take time now to pray, asking God Almighty to save you from your sins through what Jesus has done for you on the cross. He has paid the penalty for your sins. You can accept His salvation right now. Then tell a fellow group member who is a Christian or a pastor about your decision.

DAY 5

PSYCHOLOGICAL WARFARE: THE BATTLE FOR THE BELIEVER'S MIND

"Capture their minds, and their hearts and souls will follow." No one is certain who made this revealing statement about the power of psychological warfare, but it is true nonetheless. Winning the battle for the mind is essential in military campaigns. We've already learned that Paul used militaristic language to discuss his apostleship and ministry, so it should not surprise us that Paul had much to say about the battle for a Christian's mind. Spiritual warfare is won or lost primary in the psychological domain.

Our thinking can be healthy or deadly:

> Those who live according to the flesh set their minds on the things of the flesh, but those who live according to the Spirit set their minds on the things of the Spirit. For to set the mind on the flesh is death, but to set the mind on the Spirit is life and peace. For the mind that is set on the flesh is hostile to God, for it does not submit to God's law; indeed, it cannot.
> **ROMANS 8:5-7, ESV**

Is your thought life creating peace or confusion? Notice the challenge "set their minds" (v. 5, ESV). Every believer in Christ is setting his or her thinking somewhere, either on spiritual, God-centered thoughts or on unspiritual, human-centered thoughts. If our thinking is centered on the flesh, it will cause death, but if we are focused on the Spirit, we are enveloped in abundant life and peace. There is no middle ground in psychological warfare, and Satan wages a mental war to incapacitate a believer's faith.

In what specific ways do you sense that you do not use your mind to its full spiritual potential? How would you describe your thinking?

Demonic influence can cause the mind to be "hardened" (2 Cor. 3:14-15, ESV), "corrupted" (2 Tim. 3:8, ESV), "depraved" (Rom. 1:28, NIV), "blinded" in darkness (2 Cor. 4:4, ESV), "anxious" (Luke 12:29, NKJV), "shaken" (2 Thess. 2:2, NKJV), and "unstable" (Jas. 1:6-8, NKJV). It is evident that the primary target is to weaken the thought life of a believer and to corrode his or her confidence in God. These age-old psychological-warfare tactics of Satan are reminiscent of the scene in the garden of Eden, when Satan asked, "Did God really say ...?" (Gen. 3:1, NIV).

Satan never stops plotting to destroy your thinking. The Devil plays the ultimate mind games. He entices you to sin, and once you succumb to the sinful thought, he convinces you of how lousy a Christian you are. Satan has a great poker face, and he is called "the deceiver of the whole world" (Rev. 12:9, ESV). Paul warned his readers:

> ... so that we would not be outwitted by Satan;
> for we are not ignorant of his designs.
> **2 CORINTHIANS 2:11, ESV**

Many Christians fall into the trap of being outwitted, that is, cheated, by Satan. William Gurnall describes Satan's psychological warfare:

> Satan is the greatest intelligence agent in the world. He makes it his business to inquire into your inclinations, thoughts, affections and plans."[6]

There can be no compromise. Paul wrote to the Ephesians:

> This I say, therefore, and testify in the Lord, that you should
> no longer walk as the rest of the Gentiles walk, in the futility
> of their mind, having their understanding darkened.
> **EPHESIANS 4:17-18, NKJV**

If a person's mind is focused on futility, it will eventually be darkened. This is why later in the passage Paul encouraged the Ephesian Christians:

> ... to be renewed in the spirit of your minds, and
> to put on the new self, created after the likeness
> of God in true righteousness and holiness.
> **EPHESIANS 4:23-24, ESV**

A mind that is darkened is capable of unspeakable evil, and we see the results all around us. Human trafficking has become a worldwide problem, even in the United States. How could anyone abuse a small child or baby? Throughout North America repeated crimes of murder and abuse have been perpetrated against children by their own parents.

When you compare the number of hours people sit consuming television and the Internet, compared to time spent in prayer, worship, and the reading of God's Word, is there any wonder many Christians live defeated lives? Philippians 2:5 instructs us:

> Let this mind be in you which was also in Christ Jesus.
> **PHILIPPIANS 2:5, NKJV**

Resist influences in your life that could lead you to a darkened mind.

What decisions will you make to resist influences that would lead to a darkened mind? Limit the amount or type of television viewing in your home? Place stricter filters on your Wi-Fi or Internet? What else?

Satan has special methods to destroy your relationships with Christ, your spouse, your children, and those in your community. Paul tells us that we must stand against his schemes:

> … that you may be able to stand
> against the schemes of the devil.
> **EPHESIANS 6:11, ESV**

Schemes in Greek is *methodeias*, which is similar to our English word *methods*. Satan's methods are crafty, cunning, wily, and specifically designed to torment us. The good news is that with right, Christ-centric thinking we can destroy every methodical attempt of the Devil to ensnare us.

Read Matthew 22:37.

What does it mean to love the Lord your God with all your mind?

What are some specific methods Satan uses to destroy a believer's confidence in God?

The Enemy attacks male and female followers of Jesus differently. Many women struggle with identity and the sin of comparison. Satan tempts a woman to doubt herself and her identity in Christ and to think of all the ways other woman are better. A man's mind is frequently corrupted through pride. Satan uses the lust of the flesh, the lust of the eyes, and the pride of life to dismantle our character (see 1 John 2:16). Many forces can defile our minds, but one of the most seditious attacks on our thinking is pornography. Pornography can seize and stain the mind of a Christian. Paul wrote to the Philippian believers:

> Whatever is true, whatever is honorable, whatever is just, whatever is pure, whatever is lovely, whatever is commendable, if there is any excellence, if there is anything worthy of praise, think about these things.
> **PHILIPPIANS 4:8, ESV**

Over and over again, the Scriptures challenge us to renew our minds and transform our thinking. Has your mind been warped by demonic influence? What kind of thoughts do you have most often? Men, are you struggling with impure thoughts, pornography, or extramarital affairs? Young singles, are you struggling with personal purity? Women, are you wrongfully comparing yourself to others around you, setting your mind on things you do not have? What kind of mind do you have? When you are at work, what thoughts cross your mind? When you are driving alone, what things are you thinking about? As you fall asleep at night, what is on your mind? What thoughts fill your mind?

What kinds of thoughts occupy your mind most often?

A Christian's goal is to "let this mind be in you which was also in Christ Jesus" (Phil. 2:5, NKJV). "God, lead me to have the mind of Christ" should be a daily prayer request in our personal time with God. A thought is invisible, yet it can have extreme influence over our actions. We protect our minds primarily through saturation in the Word of God, worship, and ceaseless prayer. If you are struggling with a recurring sin, how many Bible verses have you memorized to motivate you to leave that sinful action behind? That is one purpose of Scripture memorization:

> Your word I have hidden in my heart,
> That I might not sin against You.
> **PSALM 119:11, NKJV**

How much time are you spending with the Word of God? The Word of God will always do the work of God in your life. When I was a young Christian, my father regularly told me, "Jeremiah, the Word will keep you from sin, or sin will keep you from the Word." I am so thankful that statement was repeatedly communicated to me through my formative years.

How much time do you devote daily to private prayer and intercession? Daily renewal of our fellowship with our Heavenly Father is necessary for strength and victory in the Christian life. Paul admonishes us in the Book of Colossians:

> Put on the new man who is renewed in knowledge
> according to the image of Him who created him.
> **COLOSSIANS 3:10, NKJV**

> Continue earnestly in prayer, being vigilant in it with thanksgiving.
> **COLOSSIANS 4:2**

How would you describe your prayer habits? What steps can you take to become more earnest and vigilant in your prayers and thanksgiving to God?

How would your prayer life change if you realized that your prayers have a renewing effect, aligning your heart and mind with God Himself?

If you are married, commit to pray daily with your spouse. I have made it my habit for many years to pray daily with Audrey. I frequently travel, and many times we are in different time zones, but we rarely miss an opportunity to pray with each other. I cannot imagine not praying with my wife, bringing to God our needs, opportunities, and challenges and listening to what He says to us.

Read engagement principle 2 in the box. Have you ever known someone who had connections to the paranormal? What spiritual needs do you sense are at the root of these practices?

What approaches would you take to guide someone involved in the paranormal to see the truth of God's Word?

Use the following scriptural directives
to guide your prayer time today.

Ask God to "lead us not into temptation, but deliver us from the evil one" (Matt. 6:13, NIV). Ask Him to give you "the mind of Christ" (1 Cor. 2:16, NIV). Ask the Lord for His strength as you seek not to be conformed "to the pattern of this world but to be transformed by the renewing of your mind" (Rom. 12:2, NIV).

■ ENGAGEMENT PRINCIPLE 2

AVOID ISLAND FEVER.

To engage, you must get out of your comfort zone. Many Christians have so isolated themselves culturally that they do not know how people who do not believe in Jesus think. Many Christians isolate themselves into irrelevancy. Jesus was intentional about seeking and developing relationships that were outside the societal norm, and we need to do the same.

Let's face it. People around us—people God has placed in our lives for his purposes—may have some crazy ideas about paranormal activity, witchcraft, zombies, demons, and other evil practices. To engage in a conversation may take you out of your comfort one, yet God has placed you in this person's life to shine light of Jesus in the darkness. This engagement principle encourages you to strongly yet sensitively and lovingly stand strong for the truth.

THE BEST SELLER NOBODY READS

HOW CAN I KNOW FOR SURE THE BIBLE IS TRUE AND TRUSTWORTHY?

JOHN 19:29

that the Scripture might be fulfilled, He said, "I'm thirsty!" 29 A jar full of sour wine was sitting there; so they fixed a sponge full of sour wine on hyssopᵃ and held it up to His mouth.
ᵃ Ps 69:21

30 When Jesus had received the sour wine, He said, ᵃ"It is finished!" Then bowing His head, He ᵇgave up His spirit.
ᵃ Jn 17:4 ᵇ Php 2:8

Jesus' Side Pierced

31 Since it was the preparation day, the Jews ᵃdid not want the bodies to remain on the cross on the Sabbath (for that Sabbath was a special day).

ously come to Him at night) also came, bringing a mixture of about 75 poundsᵉ of myrrh and aloes. 40 Then they took Jesus' body and wrapped it in linen cloths with the aromatic spices, according to the burial custom of the Jews. 41 There was a garden in the place where He was crucified. A new tomb was in the garden; no one had yet been placed in it. 42 They placed Jesus there because of the Jewish preparation and since the tomb was nearby.
ᵃ Mt 27:57 ᵇ Pr 29:25 ᶜ Jn 3:1-2 ᵈ Mt 27:60, Lk 23:53 ᵉ Is 53:9

The Empty Tomb

20 On the first day of the week Mary Magdalene came to the tomb early, while it was still dark. She saw that the stone had been removed from the tomb. 2 So she ran to Simon Peter and to the other disciple, the one Jesus loved, and said to them, "They have taken the Lord out of the tomb, and we don't know where they have put Him!"
ᵃ Mt 28:1 ᵇ Jn 13:23

3 At that, ᵃPeter and the other disciple went out, heading for the tomb. The two were running together, but the other disciple outran Peter and got to the tomb first. 5 Stooping down, he saw ᵇthe linen cloths lying there, yet he did not go in. 6 Then, following him, Simon Peter came also. He entered the tomb and saw the linen cloths lying there. 7 The wrapping that had been on His head was not lying with the linen cloths but was folded up in a separate place by itself.

START

Today's church is malnourished. Many Christians are biblically illiterate and theologically shallow. What is the Bible? Where did it come from? Was it FedExed from heaven on gold tablets? Who wrote it? Is the Bible different from other holy books? If so, how? What is the story of the Bible, anyway?

How comfortable do you feel answering a skeptic's or a new Christian's questions about the Bible?

Imagine you are explaining the Bible to someone who had never read the Bible before. How would you describe the Bible's message, meaning, and content? What makes the Bible different from any other holy book?

These are some of the questions every Christian ought to be able to answer. Unfortunately, we are living in unprecedented times of biblical illiteracy. We even have some people who are attempting to be Christians with little if any use of or appeal to the Bible. Consider the stark reality of biblical illiteracy that we face today:

- Twenty-five million new copies of the Bible are sold annually.
- Eighty percent of Americans believe the Bible is the Word of God.[1]
- The average American household owns 3 to 10 Bibles.
- Forty-two percent of American Christians say they are too busy to read the Bible.[2]
- Seventy-two percent of Americans incorrectly believe the Bible is available in all languages; in reality, over 50 percent of the world's languages still do not have a Bible translation.[3]

What is the most shocking statistic you see here? Why is it so shocking?

Mark Twain defined a classic as "a book which people praise and don't read."[4] That describes the way people view the Bible in our culture today. As Christians, we need to understand the reality of biblical illiteracy, first in our own lives and families but also in the church. Then we need to ask God for a revival of interest and commitment to the Holy Scriptures. There is work to be done, and that is why this week's study is so important.

WATCH

1. If I am in the Word of God, I will discover and implement God's will for my life.

> The KD Principle
> - Know
> - Do

> The MA Principle
> - Meaning
> - Applying

2. If I am in the Bible, it will give me strength and wisdom.

3. If I am in the Word of God, I will become convicted when there are sin and disobedience in my life.

4. If I am in the Word of God, I will successfully resist temptation and compromise in my life.

RESPOND

What one truth from Jeremiah's teaching resonated most with you?

The Bible is a love story. Actually, it is the greatest break-up-and-get-back-together story the world has ever known. The story of the Bible has a fall-in-love (God's love for us), breakup (the fall), get-back-together (Jesus and redemption) plotline. The message of the Bible is that even though we are not what we should be, God loves us, redeems us, and has a purpose for our lives.

Have you been captivated by the love story of the Bible? Have you experienced this story personally? God's Word speaks to the ultimate questions of life: Who am I? Why I am here? What are the purpose and meaning of my life?

> Blessed are those whose ways are blameless,
> who walk according to the law of the LORD.
> Blessed are those who keep his statutes
> and seek him with all their heart.
> **PSALM 119:1-2, NIV**

Have you ever experienced seasons of spiritual dryness when you were not spending time with God through His Word or seeking Him with all your heart? What was that time like, and how did you move out of that desert?

All Scripture is breathed out by God and profitable for teaching, for reproof, for correction, and for training in righteousness, that the man of God may be complete, equipped for every good work.

2 TIMOTHY 3:16-17, ESV

What is the purpose of Scripture in our lives?

Read Luke 1:1-4.

This opening to Luke's Gospel is a wonderful testimony to the careful process by which the Gospels were collated and disseminated.

How would you describe the manner in which Luke investigated, gathered, and prepared the eyewitness material of the life of Jesus?

What is the Bible to you? How would you describe it to a nonbeliever?

In this week's personal study you will be equipped with tools and answers for addressing challenging questions about the Bible.

PRAY

- Thank God for His Word.
- Pray for one another that God will speak to you through your individual study this week.
- Pray for your friends and neighbors who do not know Christ. Ask God for opportunities to talk with them about God and His Word.
- Pray for the International Bible Society and other ministries that translate and disseminate Bibles.

Read week 4 and complete the activities on the following pages before the next group experience.

DAY 1

WHAT IS THE BIBLE?

Everyone has an opinion about the Bible. Politicians attempt to use the Bible, Grammy-award winners quote the Bible, and Hollywood has portrayed the Bible on the big screen. Yet one problem remains: most people are oblivious to the Bible's basic content, meaning, and message. We say we believe in the Bible. We say we regard it as inspired and authoritative. We say we agree with the historical stance of the church that the Scriptures infallibly communicate God's truth. If this is the case, we should show the Bible some respect by knowing more about it.

All of us should be interested in biblical illiteracy, because the result of it is an increasing number of Christians who are unable to answer the unanswered questions about their faith. A lack of biblical knowledge leads to skepticism and eventual departure from the faith. It is my prayer that the tools you take from this study will equip and inspire you to present an intelligent argument for your faith, a faith in Christ that is deeply rooted in the Bible.

Mark on the continuum how would you assess your knowledge of the Bible.

1	2	3	4	5
UNCONFIDENT				VERY CONFIDENT

There is much to be learned about the Bible's history, canon, infallibility, uniqueness, and truthfulness. In what area of biblical understanding do you hope to grow most?

So what is the Bible? In some ways it is misleading to call it a *Bible*, which means *Book*. That title originated from the ancient Phoenician city of Byblos, where papyrus, which was used in making ancient scrolls and books, was sold. The Bible is really a library, a well-chosen library. We could even say the Bible is similar to an anthology of 66 volumes consisting of an Old Testament, written mostly in Hebrew (39 books), and a New Testament, written in Greek (27 books).

Read 2 Timothy 3:10-17.

According to these verses, why is Scripture is so valuable for believers?

The "Holy Scriptures" (v. 15, NIV) with which Timothy grew up were primarily the Old Testament. Yet by the time Paul wrote this letter, it is plausible that Christians considered other more recent writings to be Scripture. For example, Peter referred to Paul's writing as Scripture in 2 Peter 3:15-16.

The Bible is inspired by God. What does that mean? The Bible has a divine origin, which means the Bible's message came from God through human agency. Paul gave us a clue and a word picture in 2 Timothy 3:16: "All Scripture is given by inspiration of God" (NKJV). The English words "is given by inspiration of God" translate the Greek word *theopneustos,* which means *God-breathed* or *breathed out by God.* In this case I prefer the English Standard Version rendering of 2 Timothy 3:16: "All Scripture is breathed out by God."

■ WHAT ABOUT THE APOCRYPHA?

Old Testaments in some churches include what we call the Apocrypha. The word *Apocrypha* means *hidden* or *doubtful.* There are about 14 or 15 apocryphal books, depending on how they are counted.

For centuries Christians read the apocryphal books in addition to the 39 Old Testament books. In the 16th century Martin Luther did not recognize the apocryphal books, and as a result, our modern Bibles, which are based on Luther's Protestant canon, do not include the apocryphal writings. The Roman Catholic Church, however, maintained the status of the Apocrypha as Holy Scripture and, at the Council of Trent (1548), formally canonized them. Up to this point these books had been read and studied but not taken as seriously as the 39 books in the Old Testament. They were like an appendix to the library of the Old Testament.

These books help us understand events in Israel in the period between the Old and New Testaments. They fill in some noticeable gaps in our knowledge of the late second temple. The Books of Maccabees are especially useful in this regard. Other books, like the Wisdom of Solomon and Ecclesiasticus, help us better understand Jewish piety and the interpretation of Scripture in the generations immediately leading up to the time of Jesus.

Jerome included the apocryphal books in his Bible translation, albeit with a qualifier. He distinguished the canonical books from the helpful ecclesiastical books (or Apocrypha). Jerome described the Apocrypha as "helpful," but not "inspired."

Therefore, it is helpful for us to know what these books contain. Just because you study books outside the 66 in the Bible does not mean that you regard them as inspired Scripture or that they ought to be in the Bible.

There is another important passage in the Bible that discusses God's breath:

> The LORD God formed the man out of the dust from
> the ground and breathed the breath of life into his
> nostrils, and the man became a living being.
> **GENESIS 2:7, HCSB**

What does this comparison to the Genesis passage indicate to you about the effect God's Word can have on our lives?

When discussing 2 Timothy 3 and the inspiration of Scripture, many theologians fail to include the next verse: "that the man of God may be complete, equipped for every good work" (v. 17, ESV). Only through this infallible, God-breathed message can men and women of God be complete, using the Bible as the exclusive guide for their lives and for the practice of faith.

Just as God breathed the breath of life into a created being, God breathed into a Book. Therefore, we believe the Bible is a living Book. The Bible speaks to us as no other book can. But not everyone believes that. Many question the Bible. So how do we defend the Bible as an infallible guide for all of life? Through the rest of this week's study, you will gain critical understanding to respond with confidence to people's questions.

Record a prayer to God, thanking Him for breathing His Word
into your life through Scripture. Thank Him that His Word
gives wisdom for your life. Find one passage in the Bible
that is meaningful to you and thank Him for that as well.

DAY 2

EVIDENCE FOR THE BIBLE

"Religion is about blind faith. I would rather be scientific than blindly leap into a religious abyss." Many atheists and agnostics repeat this mantra over and again. They range from serious, respected, peer-reviewed, published scholars to nonexpert armchair atheists and agnostics.

But here is the truth. Unlike any other religion, Christianity put itself to the historical test through explicit interaction with the Roman Empire of the first century.

Have you ever heard someone state something similar to the opening quotation? How do you respond?

The miracle of the preservation of the Bible is one of the strongest forms of evidence for the veracity of Scripture. When you think about it, it is wonderful that anything from the past survives at all. For example, the Islamic State (ISIS or ISIL) is destroying countless antiquities. Statues from the classical period have been demolished, some dating to the seventh century B.C.[5] ISIS has burned books and priceless ancient manuscripts. These tragedies are occurring in our sophisticated, modern era. The Christian church was terrorized for the first three hundred years of its existence. The fact that we have any early Christian documents at all is a miracle. In comparison, Herod the Great had a secretary named Nicholas of Damascus, who wrote a *Universal History* of the ancient world in 144 volumes.[6] It is all lost. None of it survives.

SURVIVOR: HOLY SCRIPTURE

Governments have attempted to destroy the Bible for over two thousand years. Even in the English-speaking world, significant attempts have been made to usher the Bible into extinction. After John Wycliffe (c. 1331) created an uproar by translating the Latin Bible (Latin died as a lanaguge with the Roman Empire in A.D. 476) into English, it became a capital offense to translate, read, or possess an English Bible. In the fall of 1526, the bishop of London, Cuthbert Tunstall, led a massive book burning behind Saint Paul's Cathedral in an area known as Saint Paul's Cross.[7] Thousands of Bibles were lost, including precious Tyndale New Testaments.

Throughout the first three centuries of the church, the Roman government unleashed a fury on Christianity. In the days of Nero and Emperor Vespasian, edicts were issued to burn Bibles, destroy church buildings, and kill church leaders. Unparalleled in his brutality against Christians, the infamous emperor Diocletian issued an edict in 303 to destroy all Christian books and buildings. Enduring torture and death, many Christians died with their sacred writings because of their unwillingness to hand over their Scriptures to the Roman government.

In recent years skeptics have asserted that the old manuscripts on which our modern Bible translations are based are riddled with errors and are completely unreliable. (The supposed errors in the Bible will be addressed in day 3.) Many skeptics believe we cannot know what the original writers of the Bible wrote.

According to the Institute for New Testament Textual Research in Munster, Germany, we have 5,805 Greek manuscripts of the New Testament that predate the printing press. Remarkably, more than 50 of these ancient manuscripts date to before the year 300. Craig Evans recently made global headlines when he revealed that we might have a first-century fragment from the Gospel of Mark, found in a mummy mask.[8] Compared to the manuscripts of classical Greece and Rome, the New Testament evidence is quite substantial. The New Testament manuscripts are old, numerous, and reliable.

The New Testament documents are truly in a league of their own. It is remarkable how much material we have that can be quantified for the New Testament. The number, nature, and reliability of the early Christian writings are unrivaled by any literature from ancient history. And based on careful research of those documents over time, we have every reason to believe that the text of the Greek New Testament, on which our modern-language translations are based, reflects the text of the original writings of the New Testament authors. There is no basis for the idea that the books of the New Testament we have today are different in any significant way from the originals.

If we doubted what the New Testament manuscripts say about Jesus, then we must multiply those doubts a thousand times over for virtually any other classical literature and historical figure. If we were that skeptical about the New Testament, we might as well throw out 99 percent of what we know about the ancient world because we cannot rely on any of the manuscripts to tell us about it. Nobody is that skeptical.

What are your thoughts on how the Bible has survived in comparison to other ancient documents? What significance does this have for your faith in God's Word?

BACK WHEN THE CHURCH WAS TRENDY

Howard Hendricks (1924–2013), a professor at Dallas Seminary, used to say that we should charge admission for visitors at seminaries so that the world could see how people lived 50 years ago! His point was that the church is always behind the times. However, God could not have injected Jesus into the human race at a better time than in the first century, the one time in the church's history when, as Dan Wallace, the founder of the Center for the Study of New Testament Manuscripts, says, the church was "ahead of the technological curve."[9]

Have you ever wondered about the evidence for the early Christian writings? What did ancient Christian books look like? What distinguished them from other books in the ancient world? The book form everybody used until near the end of the first century was a scroll, a roll of papyrus, leather, or parchment for writing a document. In fact, the scroll was used for thousands of years prior to the New Testament. Given the ubiquity of the scroll in the Greco-Roman and Jewish traditions, we might expect early Christian books to have taken the same form. Remarkably, they did not. Almost without exception, the earliest Christian books were papyrus codices. The codex form, which is our modern book form, is bound on one side so that a reader can flip through it.

The early Christians were the first to popularize the codex format and to use it almost exclusively. In the first five hundred years after Christ, 80 percent of all Christian books were written on a codex, while only 20 percent of non-Christian books (many of which have been lost) were written in this form. The codex was not even recognized in antiquity as a proper book. Perhaps the codex—this compact book that weighed much less, was less expensive, and was easier to transport than a scroll—is one reason our Bible survived while other manuscripts did not.

How does the historical backdrop of the manuscripts of Scripture give you confidence in the reliability of your Bible?

Thank God for His perfect timing, His sovereignty over history, His protection of His Word, and His amazing love for you.

DAY 3

EVIDENCE FOR THE TEXT OF THE BIBLE

The wealth of manuscript material that is available for determining the wording of the original New Testament is striking. The New Testament is better attested than any other ancient Greco-Roman literature by far. In fact, some scholars go so far as to say the New Testament is so well evidenced that we have an embarrassment of riches. We have already discussed the fact that we have nearly 6,000 Greek manuscripts of the New Testament. What about other languages? There are over 10,000 manuscripts in Latin and somewhere between 5,000 and 10,000 manuscripts in other ancient versions like Coptic, Syriac, old-church Slavonic, Armenian, and other languages. This gives us a total of between 20,000 and 25,000 New Testament manuscripts before the invention of movable type (by Johann Gutenberg in 1454–55) or, as it is known now, the printing press.

Textual criticism (research of the text) has become one of the most important apologetic issues for the early 21st century. Textual criticism is the foundational science for investigating all literature prior to the printing press. The reason is that all manuscripts prior to the printing press had differences among themselves when compared to the original documents. This is true for the New Testament, for all classical and Greek and Roman literature, and for virtually all other ancient literature. We have to do textual criticism on these manuscripts precisely because no two manuscripts, because they are handwritten, agree with each other.

It is essential for Christians to be familiar with these issues. Christians need to be more savvy; their pastors need to be more engaged with the issues and share these issues with their people.

> In what ways should the accuracy of the Bible—that is, the inerrancy of the Bibles we have today—affect your faith?

WHAT ABOUT ALL THE "ERRORS" IN THE BIBLE?

In *Misquoting Jesus: The Story Behind Who Changed the Bible and Why* Bart Ehrman, a Bible scholar and self-identifying agnostic, makes the misleading statement that the New Testament cannot be trusted, because they are "error-ridden copies" with "200,000 variants known, some say 300,000, some say 400,000 or more!"[10] Notice that Ehrman, though a respected scholar, supports his statement with "some say ... some say."

More than 70 percent of the variants in the manuscripts of the New Testament are mere spelling differences that cannot even begin to cause confusion in how the original text might have read. That is significant. Almost all the remaining variants involve minor changes. Less than 1 percent of all the textual variants have any consequence on the text, and none of these variants affect what we know about Jesus, the gospel, or the early church.

■ HOW RELIABLE ARE THE BIBLICAL DOCUMENTS?

Both the quantity and the quality of the manuscripts of the Scriptures give us confidence in the Bible's accuracy. Although no original manuscripts of Old Testament books exist, scribes took painstaking efforts to preserve the Old Testament books by copying them by hand.

The Dead Sea Scrolls, discovered in 1947, provided us a Hebrew text dating from the second century B.C. Including all Old Testament books except Esther, the Dead Sea Scrolls confirm the reliability of ancient manuscript copies of the Old Testament.

Another important discovery was the pre-Christian Greek version of the Old Testament called the Septuagint, produced from about 285 to 270 B.C. This version is frequently quoted in the New Testament because it served as the Bible of Greek-speaking Christians in the apostolic period. Scholars have also used this text to confirm the accuracy of Hebrew versions of the Old Testament.[11]

No book in ancient literature can compare with the New Testament in documentary support. About 24,000 manuscripts exist—5,664 in Greek; 8,000 to 10,000 in Latin; and 8,000 in Ethiopic, Slavic, and Armenian. In contrast, we have only 7 ancient copies of Plato's writings, 5 of Aristotle's, and 643 of Homer's.

The New Testament manuscripts are not only numerous but also very early. Approximately 75 papyri fragments date from the early second to the mid-eighth century A.D., covering 25 of the 27 New Testament books. One fragment of the Book of John has been dated as early as A.D. 100. We therefore possess New Testament manuscripts dating within a couple of generations after the originals were written. In contrast, the oldest existing manuscripts of most nonbiblical books date from 8 or 10 centuries after the original works were written. For example, the oldest manuscript of Caesar's Gallic War, composed between 58 and 56 B.C., dates from about 900 years after Caesar's day.[12]

The quality of the New Testament manuscripts is without parallel. Because of the great reverence the early Christians had for the Scriptures, they exercised extreme caution in accurately copying and preserving the authentic text. No discrepancies among texts call into question a major doctrine or factual teaching.[13]

Yet assertions like those of Bart Ehrman present pitfalls for unprepared believers. Some Christians hear these sound bites and assume the Bible was corrupted and cannot be trusted. Christians hear the number 400,000, along with a few examples of the meaningful and viable variants, and conclude that they have no idea what the original text said and the whole thing must be corrupted. Unfortunately, some Christians have given up on the Christian faith because they read claims from books like *Misquoting Jesus* without understanding the evidence for the Bible.

We need to give the ancient scribes more credit. They were careful, studious, and committed to faithfully transmitting the Scriptures. Recently, Dan Wallace was presenting a guest lecture to my students when he shared about an expedition to Athens, where he and his team at the Center for the Study of New Testament Manuscripts were photographing New Testament manuscripts at the National Library of Greece. To conclude his lecture, Dan presented a colophon (a note written by a scribe at the end of a manuscript) highlighting the care one scribe took in his work:

> The hand that wrote [this] is rotting in the grave. But the letters
> remain until the fullness of time. Completed with [the help of] God.
> February 23, Friday, the second hour, during the eleventh indiction,
> in the year 1079, through the hand of Andrew, scribe, and calligra-
> pher. And if it happens that any error of omission [remains]—this,
> for the sake of Christ, forgive me.[14]

Do variants in the manuscripts alter our understanding of Jesus, undermine what He said or did, or challenge a significant doctrine of the church? Absolutely not. The legendary text critic Bruce Metzger was asked a similar question, and his response settles the question: "The more significant variations do not overthrow any doctrine of the church."[15] Metzger went on to say that his decades studying the ancient manuscripts of the Bible had increased the vibrancy of his faith:

> It has increased the basis of my personal faith to see the firmness
> with which these materials have come down to us, with a multiplicity
> of copies, some of which are very ancient, … and today I know with
> confidence that my trust in Jesus has been well placed.[16]

How would you respond to someone who tells you the Bible is full of errors because it has been copied over and over throughout thousands of years?

Pray today for people you know who struggle with the accuracy, validity, and inerrancy of the Bible. Ask God, through His Spirit, to guide them toward His truth (see John 16:13) and to draw them to Himself.

DAY 4

MEMORY, ORALITY, AND THE REAL JESUS

Bible skeptics often make two opposing claims:

1. The Gospels must not be accurate, because it took 30 to 40 years for the eyewitnesses to write them down.

2. We can learn more about the historical Jesus from sources other than the New Testament Gospels, sources written in the second and third centuries or even later.

Have you heard either one of these claims? Do you have any immediate reaction to either or both of these statements? If so, explain.

HOW DID THE NEW TESTAMENT WRITERS REMEMBER WHAT JESUS SAID AND DID?

How did Matthew remember the Sermon on the Mount and accurately record it in his Gospel? How did Dr. Luke transcribe the words of Peter's Pentecost sermon in Acts? How could the writers remember everything for so many years before it was recorded? We believe the Gospels are eyewitness accounts. Why did the eyewitnesses take 30 to 40 years to write their accounts?

These are great questions, but the very fact that these questions are raised reflects a modern way of thinking. We are looking at the New Testament through 21st-century glasses.

How is information most commonly passed along in today's culture? How could these methods be different from the means used in the first century?

If the president of the United States says something, you can read it almost immediately on Twitter, on the Internet, or in a newspaper. It would seem strange to us if somebody said, "Someone will write down the President's speech in about 20 years. But for now we'll just pass it along by word of mouth."

We live in an age of instant information. What is happening in the world is literally at our fingertips. But that was not Jesus' world. When Jesus spoke in the first century, His purpose was not for someone to record His words. He taught, repeated His message, and expressed His teachings using new words in a new context. In doing so, He showed that the message was adaptable, and He expected His disciples to learn it, repeat it, and apply it in their own ways. Jesus did not write down His sermon and then read it. That is a modern approach.

The first century, then, was an oral culture. That is the way things were done. People were used to listening to what someone taught and remembering it. In an oral culture the verbal story of someone who experienced an event had more value than the written word; it was seen as a living voice.

Why did it take so long for the Gospels to be written? People did not start writing them down until these witnesses, these living voices, began to die. They realized that soon they would not have the eyewitnesses around to tell the stories orally. So they began to write the stories down.

The apostles oversaw this oral tradition. When Judas was replaced, the requirement was that the new apostle had to be someone who had been with Jesus from the beginning. He had to have know Jesus personally.

We know from Scripture that Jesus taught the Sermon on the Mount, but He probably taught the same type of message frequently as He traveled from place to place. His followers would have heard this teaching over and over, remembered it, and eventually memorialized it in writing as eyewitnesses began to die off.

Read Acts 4:20.

What does Peter and John's response signify to you about the oral culture in which they lived?

WHERE DO WE FIND THE REAL, HISTORICAL JESUS?

Many pseudoscholarly professors, popular writers, and movie makers want us to believe that our best sources for the historical Jesus are not Matthew, Mark, Luke, and John. The person these men portray is not the real Jesus, they say. We have been fed all kinds of strange ideas, many of which have already been disproved. Truthfully, much of this stuff is beyond belief.

Some of these modern portraits of Jesus are based on the extracanonical Gospels, and invariably the Jesus that emerges is not the Christ of the Bible, not the Christ proclaimed by the apostles, and not the Christ of the faith of the early church. These extracanonical Gospels are late, nonapostolic, and idiosyncratic, and they do not accurately depict the first-century world of Jesus.

Dan Brown, the Jesus Seminar, hyperskeptical scholars, and others in their company have it all wrong because they use questionable sources. The Jesus Seminar's work is flawed because it has leaned heavily on some of these sources, and it has measured the first-century New Testament Gospels in the light of these sources.

If you want the real Jesus, He can be found in first-century apostolic writings. If you are doing historical work, don't you want the earliest sources? If you are talking about somebody who said remarkable things and did astounding things, don't you want to talk to the people who saw Him, knew Him, and heard Him?

It would be very difficult to talk about life 150 years ago. If you decided to write a journal pretending to be somebody who lived in the 1850s, you would probably make mistakes because you are not exactly sure how day-to-day living took place. You would slip up. These extracanonical Gospel writers slipped up many times. When the four Gospel writers talked about the real Jesus in the 20s and 30s, they did not slip up.

Read John 20:30-31; 21:24-25.

What do these verses teach you about the trustworthiness of these eyewitness writers?

Read John 14:25-26; 16:12-13.

What do these passages add to your reasons to trust these eyewitness accounts?

Close your study time today by thanking God for His life-giving Scriptures. Ask Him to guide you as you learn to appreciate and study His Word.

DAY 5

THE REAL, HISTORICAL JESUS

How do we find the real Jesus and transcend all the distortions being tossed around in our culture? Let's look at what the real Jesus taught, did, and achieved.

WHAT DID THE REAL JESUS TEACH?

In the real Gospels—the first-century Gospels—you discover that Jesus proclaimed the kingdom of God. He said that this kingdom had come and that it makes a difference for eternity. You will not find that teaching in the Gospel of Thomas, the Gospel of Peter, or some of these other writings. You certainly won't find it in any of the Gospels that were not included in the New Testament canon.

The real Jesus taught that He is more powerful than Satan, and He demonstrated it with exorcisms. Jesus taught that One wiser and greater than Solomon was here. Solomon was famous in the Jewish world of Jesus' time, so that was an amazing claim.

Jesus taught that He had authority to forgive sin; that is an amazing claim. "Who is this man who even forgives sins?" (Luke 7:49, HCSB), the Pharisees asked. That is someone with authority from heaven. That is what the four Gospels teach. That is what the real Jesus taught.

In your mind what are some of the more radical claims Jesus made?

WHAT DID THE REAL JESUS DO?

Jesus reached out and forgave sinners. He summoned and empowered disciples. He challenged the calloused and indifferent. He rebuked hypocrites and phonies. He warned apostates of coming judgment. He surrendered His life in order to fulfill the will of His Father in heaven.

You will not find the Jesus who did those things in any of the extracanonical Gospels. In fact, you will discover that sin is no big deal in these other Gospels. Sin is no big deal in some circles today as well, and that is why many people today are attracted to these Gospels. They mirror the thinking of a lot of people today. Not everybody wants Jesus to be Lord. Not everyone wants to be held accountable. The phony Jesus claimed by many people today is a much-compromised Jesus.

> Read Mark 1:21-22; 2:1-17. What do these verses reveal to you about the following traits of the real Jesus?

> The focus of His heart:

> The way He treated sin:

> His authority:

WHAT DID THE REAL JESUS ACHIEVE?

Jesus revealed the true God in His fullness. "Anyone who has seen me has seen the Father" (John 14:9, NIV), He explained to His disciples. The real Jesus died on the cross for sinners, making forgiveness possible.

The Jesus of the extracanonical Gospels did not die on the cross. There is no talk of forgiveness of sin; in fact, these Gospels go out of their way to suggest that something else happened. The second-century heretic Basilides suggested that Jesus fooled everybody by trading places with Simon of Cyrene.

Talk about having a bad day! According to Basilides, Simon of Cyrene showed up for the Passover, and the next thing he knew, he was asked to carry Jesus' cross. Jesus then slipped away in the crowd, and everybody thought Simon was Jesus. So poor Simon was nailed to the cross, and Jesus sneaked away laughing.

As crazy as that story may sound, a similar story is repeated in the Qur'an today. That's why Muslims say Jesus was not put to death by the Jews.

The real Jesus of the New Testament Gospels was crucified, died a real death, and was raised in a real resurrection on the third day, thus confirming all He taught and proving that His life and death were approved by God. His sacrifice was indeed acceptable. And it would not need to be repeated. That is what the real Jesus achieved.

The phony Jesus did none of those things. The phony Jesus offers no hope. In fact, the phony Jesus is quite diverse. There are all kinds of phony Jesuses.

Read Luke 24:36-53.

This passage shows what Jesus achieved for His first disciples and for us. They were personal eyewitnesses of these things (see v. 48).

What has Jesus achieved in your life that makes you a witness for Him?

Read engagement principle 3 in the box. Considering the evidence you've studied this week about God's Word, what approach would you take to engage with someone who doubted the trustworthiness of the Bible?

As you close, look again at Luke 24:52-53. Jesus' disciples responded to everything they had witnessed with worship and great joy. Reflect on your own response to the real Jesus—the Jesus of the New Testament Gospels. Record your response to Him.

■ ENGAGEMENT PRINCIPLE 3

Be cool. The more you know, the more relaxed you should be.

Too many Christians prepare for a faith conversation as if they were preparing for war: attack! This approach is the exact opposite of what we see in the life of Christ. We need to strengthen our ability to begin comfortable faith conversations, not a debate or battle, succinctly and confidently sharing why Jesus is our hope and the Bible is our authoritative guide for living.

One purpose of this study is to provide us with more knowledge about our faith. This week's personal study has included information about the Bible so that as we engage in discussions, we will know what we are talking about. When we have tools and answers like those presented in this study, we will not need to retreat or shy away from tackling tough questions. We can relax and confidently stand up for the truth of God's Word.

As you gain confidence and learn to answer unanswered questions, you will feel more comfortable and relaxed in any faith dialogue. Your goal is a posture that is peaceful and cool.

JOHN 19:29

...that the Scripture might be fulfilled, He said, "I'm thirsty!" [29] A jar full of sour wine was sitting there; so they fixed a sponge full of sour wine on hyssop[a] and held it up to His mouth.

[a] Ps 69:21

[30] When Jesus had received the sour wine, He said, [a]"It is finished!" Then bowing His head, He [b]gave up His spirit.

[a] Jn 17:4 [b] Php 2:8

Jesus' Side Pierced

[31] [a]Since it was the preparation day, the Jews [b]did not want the bodies to [...]th on the cross on the Sabbath [...] Sabbath was [c]a special[b] day). [...]equested that Pilate have the [...]gs broken and that their bod[...]en away. [32] So the [...] [...] for one [...] who had [...] Jesus. [33] Then to [...] [...]Jesus, they did not break His [...]ce they saw that He was already [...] But one of the soldiers pierced [...] with [a] spear, and [...] once [...] and water [...]ame out. [35] He who [...] has te[...]fied [...] [...]eve. His testimony is true, and [...] he is telling the truth. [36] For [...] things happened [a]so that the [...]pture would be fulfilled: Not one [c]f His bones will be broken. [37] Also, [...]other Scripture says: [g]They will [...]ok at the One they pierced.[d]

[a] Mk 15:42 [b] Dt 21:23 [c] Ex 12:18
[d] Zch 13:1 [e] Jn 20:31 [f] 1Jn 1:1
[f] Ex 12:46 [f] Ps 34:20 [g] Zch 12:10

[...] After this, Joseph of Arimathea [...] cretly [b]because of his fear of the Jews—asked Pilate that he might remove Jesus' body. Pilate gave him permission, so he came and took His body away. [39] [e]Nicodemus (who had previ-

ously come to Him at night) also came, bringing a mixture of about 75 pounds[e] of myrrh and aloes. [40] Then they took Jesus' body and wrapped it in linen cloths with the aromatic spices, according to the burial custom of the Jews. [41] There was a garden in the place where He was crucified. A [d]new tomb was in the garden; no one had yet been placed in it. [42] [e]They placed Jesus there because of the Jewish preparation and since the tomb was nearby. [a] Mt 27:57 [b] Pr 29:25 [c] Jn 3:1-2
[d] Mt 27:60; Lk 23:53 [e] Is 53:9

The Empty Tomb

20 On the [a]first day of the week [...] Mary Magdalene came to the tomb early, while it was still dark. She [...] the stone [...]d been re[...]ved [...] the tomb, [...] she ran to[...]mon [...]er and to [...] other disci[...] [...] Jesus loved, and said to them, "They have taken the Lord out of the tomb, and we don't know where they [...] put [...] [b] Jn 13:23 [...] [...] Peter [...] the [...]er disci-[...]ple [...] [...]g [...]e tomb. [4] The two were running together, but the other disciple outran Peter and got to the tomb first. [5] Stooping down, he saw [b]the linen cloths lying there, yet he did not go in. [6] Then, following him, Simon Peter came also. He entered the tomb and saw the linen cloths lying there. [7] The wrapping that had been on His head was not lying with the linen cloths but was folded [...] separate place by itself. [8] [...]he [...] disciple, who had reached the [...] first [...] [...]saw and believed. [9] For they still did not understand the Scripture that He must rise from the dead. [10] Then the disciples went home again.

[a] Lk 24:12 [b] Jn 19:40
[a] Ps 16:10; Mt 16:21

WEEK 5

INVISIBLE ILLNESS

WHAT SHOULD CHRISTIANS UNDERSTAND ABOUT SUICIDE AND MENTAL HEALTH?

Reat and manifold were the bleſſings (m[...]
Soueraigne) which Almightie God, th[...]
of all Mercies, beſtowed vpon vs the p[...]
ENGLAND, when firſt hee ſent your [...]
Royall perſon to rule and raigne ouer v[...]
whereas it was the expectation of man[...]
wiſhed not well vnto our Sion[...]

START

Kim was in the prime of her life and was a devout Christian who regularly attended our church. She was married, the mother of four beautiful children, a lover of animals, and a nominee for teacher of the year. However, Kim, age 43, struggled with chronic depression. One day, seeing no way out of her desolation, she went into the woods and committed suicide. The family asked me to officiate and give the message at Kim's funeral service. I also worked with the family to try and pick up the pieces. The *why* questions will never end. My experience with Kim and her family awakened me to the stark reality of mental illness—the invisible illness—in our church families.

How aware and prepared do you think the church is to deal with the reality of suicide and mental health?

Consider the following statistics on suicide.

- Worldwide nearly a million people commit suicide each year.[1]
- Globally, one person dies every 40 seconds by his or her own hand.[2]
- Every 15 minutes someone commits suicide in the United States.[3]
- Twice as many U.S. citizens kill themselves than kill one another each year, proving that we are far more dangerous to ourselves than to other people.
- One in five suicides in the United States is a war veteran.[4]
- Males take their lives at nearly five times the rate of females and represent more than 80 percent of all U.S. suicides.[5]

Suicide has reached epidemic levels. Yet suicide is preventable. Unfortunately, most people do not know where to start.

What goes through your mind as you hear these statistics?

In this session we will address two topics of great consequence to us as humans and especially as Christ's church: suicide and mental illness. The church has generally avoided conversations at the intersection of faith, suicide, and mental illness. It is time to ask ourselves, *What would Christ want us to do?*

WATCH

1. Stop the silence.

2. Stop the shame and exclusion.

3. Understand mental illness and be present.

4. Be part of the equation treating mental illness.

THE HEALING EQUATION

1. Admit every family struggles.

2. Love instead of judge, condemn, and misunderstand.

3. Build support groups for every age level in our church for addressing mental disorders.

4. Encourage the mentally ill in our church communities to serve.

RESPOND

What one truth from Jeremiah's teaching resonated most with you?

Let's humbly investigate God's Word to learn what it has to say about suicide and to discover ways we can respond well to anyone affected by mental illness or suicidal thoughts.

Read Romans 8:35-39.

What does this passage reveal about our value to God?

How can you apply this passage to the experience of someone who deals with mental illness or suicide thoughts?

Until you have been brought to the brink, you may not understand the intensity of another individual's struggle that might trigger a suicide attempt. God knows the internal struggles of our hearts. The promise of Romans 8 is that when we commit our lives to Christ, nothing can separate us from His love.

Individuals attempt suicide for many reasons, and we often never know why. However, we do know how much God values human life. He created us to have an abundant life; however, we have an Enemy who, "like a roaring lion" (1 Pet. 5:8, ESV), has come into the world to "steal and kill and destroy" our lives (John 10:10, ESV).

Read the following passages. Discuss what each one teaches us about protecting ourselves and having the mind of Christ. How can these verses help people who are dealing with mental illness and suicidal thoughts?

> Above all else, guard your heart,
>   for everything you do flows from it.
> **PROVERBS 4:23, NIV**

> Do not conform to the pattern of this world, but
> be transformed by the renewing of your mind.
> Then you will be able to test and approve what
> God's will is—his good, pleasing and perfect will.
> **ROMANS 12:2, NIV**

> We demolish arguments and every pretension that sets
> itself up against the knowledge of God, and we take
> captive every thought to make it obedient to Christ.
> **2 CORINTHIANS 10:5, NIV**

In this week's personal study we will seek to understand more about suicide and mental illnesses. We will investigate these topics and explore what the Bible says about them so that we can answer our own questions, as well as those of people who are suffering from these invisible illnesses.

PRAY

- Begin your prayer time by recognizing God's presence with you and your absolute dependence on and security in Him as you explore these topics.
- Thank God for life, both the abundant life he makes available now and the eternal life He has provided through Jesus.
- Pray specifically and compassionately for individual group members' needs, especially as related to suicide and mental illness.

Read week 5 and complete the activities on the following pages before the next group experience.

DAY 1

MENTAL ILLNESS

No one is unaffected by mental illness. If you have not personally struggled with mental illness, chances are that your friend, spouse, child, coworker, or neighbor has. As Christians, we need to build awareness of the problem and remove the stigma, because mental illness is widespread and affects everyone. The ministry of Jesus focused on removing barriers to belief and restoring people who were suffering. The church needs to follow His example. Yet a LifeWay Research survey found that 66 percent of pastors rarely or never address the subject of mental illness from their pulpits. And the same survey revealed that the majority of churchgoers wish their pastors would talk about it.[6]

When you read the words *mental illness*, what pictures or words immediately come into your mind?

Many stigmatize the mentally ill as people in hospital gowns committed deep inside a psych ward. But that is a very inaccurate depiction of someone with a mental illness. Would it surprise you to learn that people with mental illnesses worship at your church and probably attend your Bible-study group with you?

It is very sad that we say so little about mental illness in the church. We act as if it does not exist. Rarely do we hear sermons or read Bible-study material on this topic. It has left some Christian leaders in a quandary because in almost every family, at least one person is suffering from mental illness.

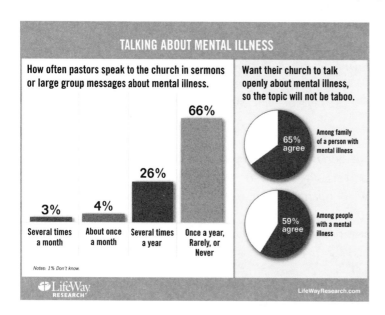

TALKING ABOUT MENTAL ILLNESS

How often pastors speak to the church in sermons or large group messages about mental illness.

3% Several times a month
4% About once a month
26% Several times a year
66% Once a year, Rarely, or Never

Notes: 1% Don't know.

LifeWay RESEARCH

Want their church to talk openly about mental illness, so the topic will not be taboo.

65% agree — Among family of a person with mental illness

59% agree — Among people with a mental illness

LifeWayResearch.com

Why do you suspect the church says so little about mental illness?

One article summarized the findings of the LifeWay Research study and further added that "Nearly 1 in 4 pastors (23 percent) acknowledge they have 'personally struggled with mental illness,' and half of those pastors said the illness had been diagnosed, according to the poll."[7]

Are you surprised by the statistics about pastors and mental illnesses? Why or why not?

◼ 10 PRIORITIES OF MENTALLY HEALTHY LEADERS

My friend (and professor at Midwestern Baptist Theological Seminary) Dr. Larry Cornine founded the Diakonos Counseling Center. After 30 years of treating pastors and professionals, he presented a top-10 list for mental health in his courses. Whether you are the pastor of a church, a small-group leader, a business professional, or a leader in your family, these 10 directives will encourage stability and mental health in your life.

1. Say no more often.
2. Take frequent short sabbaticals.
3. Develop and sustain peer support; maintain an active relationship with an accountability partner.
4. Monitor your balance between work and personal life.
5. Establish and adjust priorities based on a periodic review of your personal values.
6. Proof your thoughts against Scripture.
7. Regularly assess your spiritual fitness.
8. Do not make decisions when you are tired.
9. Prioritize your physical health: eat nutritiously, be physically active, and get adequate sleep and rest.
10. Watch where you park your mind.

AS WE WAIT

So what do we do with this information? If I could give one overarching piece of advice, it would be to wait. Wait patiently for God.

God's people have always been a people who waited. In Old Testament times faithful Jews waited for the Messiah to come to earth, and today we wait for His second coming, when He will make all things new (see Rev. 21:5). At that time we as believers will be with God in a place where …

> There will be no more death or mourning or crying
> or pain, for the old order of things has passed away.
> **REVELATION 21:4, NIV**

Until Christ comes again, as we wait, we "groan inwardly" (Rom. 8:23, NIV) in these present sufferings. We are weak in body and mind, but we have an incredible promise and gift: "the Spirit helps us in our weakness" (v. 26, NIV).

Read Romans 8:18-26.

Pastor and blogger Stephen Altrogge put it like this:

> Until the day Jesus returns, I will live in a body which does not function as God originally intended. My brain, which is a key, central, integral part of my body, will not function correctly. Chemicals will become imbalanced. Serotonin will not be properly absorbed. Norepinephrine will be unevenly distributed. Synapses won't fire correctly. My brain, just like every other part of my body, is prone to illness. [8]

How does God's perspective from Romans 8 and Revelation 21 affect your thoughts and feelings about mental illness?

Pray today for anyone you know who is affected by
mental illness. Ask for God's blessings and strength
in their lives. Pray that God will show you how to be
involved in this person's life to love and care for them.

DAY 2

A PLACE FOR GRACE TO SHINE

One of the most popular movies of 2015 was *American Sniper,* based on the life of Chris Kyle, a sniper who set records in the number of kills while in combat. After four tours in Iraq, this married father of two clearly experienced psycho-logical fallouts from battle stress, or posttraumatic stress disorder (PTSD). As he tried to insert himself back into everyday life, he sometimes had bad dreams or flashbacks from battle. A patient wife and a wise physician directed Chris to help other marines by listening to their wartime stories and, in many cases, observing the physical and emotional handicaps they inherited from severe, nightmarish combat missions and the death of their comrades in battle. Chris was recovering when, at a shooting range, a former marine who was mentally ill, Eddie Ray Routh, turned the gun on America's most heroic sniper and killed him and his close friend, Chad Littlefield.

God clearly teaches throughout Scripture that we are called to minister to the weak and sick, including those with mental sickness. Let's focus today on how grace can shine through us into the lives of people who are struggling with mental illness.

■ A STARK REALITY

- Depression is the leading cause of disability.[9]
- In 2012 there were an estimated 9.6 million adults age 18 or older in the United States who had serious mental illness in the past year.
- In 2012 there were an estimated 43.7 million adults age 18 and older in the United States with a mental illness in the past year. This means one in five adult Americans suffers from a mental illness.
- Just more than 20 percent of children, either currently or at some point during their lives, have had serious debilitating mental disorders.
- Major depression is one of the most common disorders in the United States.

- One in 20 Americans lives with serious mental illness: bipolar, schizophrenia, PTSD, or chronic depression.
- In 2012 an estimated 16 million adults age 18 or older in the United States had at least one major depressive episode in the past year.
- In 2012 an estimated 2.2 million adolescents ages 12 to 17 in the United States had at least one major depressive episode in the past year.
- Forty-eight percent—nearly half the world's population—will have a direct experience with mental illness themselves over the course of their lifetimes.[10]

As you read these statistics, what kind of biblical principles come to mind in regard to your responsibility for those affected by mental illness?

Read the following verse and record how each speaks to our responsibility to care for individuals with mental illness.

Psalm 82:4

Acts 20:35

Galatians 6:2

Philippians 2:4

Think about someone you know who has been affected by posttraumatic stress or other psychological fallouts from war, a natural disaster, a crash, abuse, the sudden death of a loved one, or another traumatic experience. In what ways can you minister to this person and show God's grace?

WHAT CAUSES MENTAL ILLNESSES?

Invisible illnesses of the brain have the power to isolate you, kill you, shorten your lifespan, and cause you to cease to be a productive member of society. Mental illness is not a choice, but the good news is that it is treatable. The Bible says we were born in sin:

> Through one man sin entered the world, and death through sin, and thus death spread to all men, because all sinned.
> **ROMANS 5:12, NKJV**

We inherit a curse from Adam that manifests itself in the human body in many ways. The body grows old; strength dissipates; and eventually, our immune systems cannot fight off diseases. Our cell structure breaks down, and eventually, we expire. We are prone to do wrong. Character is not natural, but sin is. In a strange way that not even the best mental professionals can fully explain, many people experience mental illness.

Studies indicate that in some cases mental illness is biological and perhaps even generational. In other instances severe psychological trauma triggered by harrowing, unexpected, extremely difficult circumstances in life have induced mental illness. And of course, in the backdrop of all illness is daily spiritual war (see Eph. 6:10-18) being waged by the Devil (see John 8:44) and his myriad of demons working to cause Christians to fail. Therefore, we must be discerning enough to determine whether the errant or odd behavior in a person is sin or something induced by a mental illness. Thank God for the growing number of trained, licensed, board-certified specialists in the mental-health vocation who are Christians and understand these competing factors.

Think for a moment about a physical illness or weakness you have. In what ways are mental illnesses the same as or different from physical ones?

Read Matthew 9:35-36.

Notice two important points in this passage. First, Jesus healed every disease and sickness. Jesus has the power to heal all kinds of infirmities—physical, psychological, emotional, and spiritual. Second, don't miss what caused Jesus to heal these people: his compassion for them. Our ministry to "harassed and helpless" people (v. 36, NIV)—and those words certainly describe many people with mental illnesses—begins with compassionate hearts.

■ COMMON MENTAL-HEALTH DISORDERS

DEPRESSION is a precursor to suicide if not treated.

ANXIETY DISORDERS reflect 18 percent of U.S. adults and 25 percent of 13- to 18-year-olds.

POSTTRAUMATIC STRESS DISORDER (PTSD) is an anxiety disorder that can develop after exposure to a terrifying event or situation.

BIPOLAR DISORDER, sometimes referred to as manic-depressive disorder, is characterized by dramatic shifts in mood, energy, and activity levels. It hinders a person's day-to-day ability to function and carry out responsibilities.

SCHIZOPHRENIA is a chronic, severe, and disabling mental disorder demonstrated by deficits in thought processes, perceptions, and emotional responsiveness. In some instances schizophrenics can become violent, attack, and kill. Because their brain processes do not function properly, they can imagine people as fictional characters and conjure all kinds of paranoia—often the driving impulse to retaliate.

As Christians, as Jesus' hands and feet on earth, we have the responsibility and privilege to help people who are dealing with sin in their lives. At the same time, we cannot assume that sin is the problem. We must understand that there are differences among spiritual struggles, weaknesses, and mental illness. So we also have the opportunity to bring comfort and encouragement in people's weaknesses and to care for them in their mental illnesses. Be aware of what you have the knowledge and ability to do and when it is time to refer a person to a trained professional for help.

Most important, allow God to change your heart to be more like Christ in His compassion and care for harassed, helpless people. His grace can shine through you into the lives of people with mental illness.

As you close today, reflect for a few minutes about your heart and attitudes toward people with mental illnesses. Is there anything you need to repent of? Are there any attitudes you need to allow God's Spirit to convict you of? Do you need to ask Jesus to give you the same kind of compassion for people that He had? Ask God to use you to be His hands and feet to people with mental illnesses.

DAY 3

THE MENTALLY ILL AND YOU

Daniel Morehead, a Christian psychiatrist, said at the Leadership Network's Mental Health and the Church summit:

> Mental illness is not a matter of choice or willpower. It is a matter of can't rather than won't.[11]

There is hope for every person who suffers from mental illness. In some cases God has healed individuals of these disorders due to fervent prayer and God's perfect will. In other cases, after years of prayer and ministry, the mentally ill person has remained unchanged and often propelled deeper into their illness, creating family havoc and worry by parents, grandparents, spouses, and friends.

Read 1 John 4:15-19.

> What are two or three specific ways you can personally demonstrate love to someone with a mental illness?

Look again at verse 18. This verse reminds us that God is greater than any fears or other problems we may face in life. However, this verse is not written as a judgment on anxiety disorders. Although God's Word is truth, as Christians, we must be careful not to use it to judge or as an easy fix for deep-seated issues.

It is easy to tell someone the Bible says not to worry (see Matt. 6:25) or to pray rather than be anxious (see Phil. 4:6), but such platitudes rarely help a hurting person. It is much more costly to care for someone, to listen without judgment, and to minister to their needs, but these things are far more helpful. Consider this. Would you scold or throw out-of-context Bible verses at a person with a broken bone or a case of pneumonia?

> Read the following verses and record ways you can apply each verse in ministry to a person with mental illness. Be as specific as possible.
>
> Romans 14:13
>
> Romans 15:7
>
> Ephesians 4:2
>
> James 5:16

WAYS TO MINISTER TO PEOPLE WITH INVISIBLE DISEASES

Use the following Spirit-led steps yourself or in your church, small group, or class to minister to people with mental illnesses.

- Start the conversation. Remove the stigma. Stop the isolation.
- Provide specific ministry for those suffering from mental illness in the church. This is best accomplished through private recovery groups in which those who are living with the same mental illness can gain new friendships and greater understanding.
- Faithfully and fervently pray for these individuals, believing God can do the impossible. With this godly ambition we must pray for God's perfect will to be accomplished (see 1 John 5:14-15).
- Find a qualified biblically based counselor or mental-health professional who can bring further insight to those suffering from mental illness.
- Emphasize the power of God's Word to heal the mind, heart, and soul.
- Read and study the Bible. God's Word is therapeutic for all of us. It is inspired by the Holy Spirit and can calm us in the greatest crisis (see Heb. 4:12). Read Scripture aloud in your home. Read the Bible when your thoughts are troubled and anxiety seeks to bind you. Watch for ways the Holy Spirit uses the Bible to comfort you in every life situation.

Which one or two of these methods will you implement first to minister to someone with mental illness? Outline a plan for doing so. Include whom it will involve, what steps you need to take, and what your time frame will be.

We live in challenging days, but we can stay encouraged by calling on the power of the blood of Jesus Christ and by relying on prayers of intercession by our fellow believers.

Pray today that God will move and equip you, your group, and your church to reach out to and lovingly, compassionately minister to people with mental illness.

DAY 4

THE EPIDEMIC OF SUICIDE

"Another Pastor Commits Suicide" is a headline that, unfortunately, is becoming more prevalent.[12] Pastor Robert took his life the week following the Sunday he preached on Romans 8:28:

> We know that all things work together for good to those who love God, to those who are called according to His purpose.
> **ROMANS 8:28, NKJV**

Pastor Robert was described as an incredibly gifted teacher of God's Word. He seemed to conceal his suicidal inclination until the April day in 2014 when he hanged himself. The church he pastored reflected on his ministry in a eulogy by lamenting that although he had a passion to heal broken people through Jesus Christ, he had been unable to find peace for his own brokenness.

Tragically, there have been scores of deaths by suicide throughout North America. It is rare that people outside the immediate family discover all the personal facts behind a person's suicide. Family members, in anguish, grief, and utter sympathy, seldom disclose all the intricacies and challenges of the deceased person's life. Some suicides seem like a riddle and have no logical meaning. Most leave us with the searing question, Why?

■ FACTS ABOUT SUICIDE

- Globally, one person dies every 40 seconds by his or her own hand.[13]
- One million people worldwide take their lives each year.[14]
- Every 15 minutes someone commits suicide in the United States.[15]
- Twice as many U.S. citizens kill themselves than kill one another each year.
- One in five completed suicides in the United States involves a war veteran.[16]
- Suicide rates for females are highest among those ages 45 to 54.

- Males take their lives at nearly five times the rate of females and represent more than 80 percent of all U.S. suicides.[17]
- Suicide is the second-leading cause of death among college students.[18]
- Suicide is the third-leading cause of death among those ages 15 to 24.[19]
- Suicide is the fourth-leading cause of death among those ages 10 to 14.
- For every person who takes his or her life, there are 25 attempted suicides.

Examine the statistics in the box on the previous page. What facts strike you as particularly surprising or troubling?

When you hear about a suicide, especially when it involves a pastor or his family, what questions do you have?

Far too often, the average Christian feels ill equipped to respond to a suicide. People who die by suicide leave family members and friends in a state of emotional and spiritual shock. In fact, those left behind frequently react by doubting God and asking why He allowed this to happen. That question almost has the implied tone "Why did God do this?" This is an understandable query, but it overlooks the fact that God created people with free will. Further, such a response omits an understanding of the facts involved in suicide.

CAN A CHRISTIAN COMMIT SUICIDE?

The obvious answer is yes. A Christian can commit any sin know to man. In disobedience they can steal, murder, lie, and grieve the Lord in any number of ways. But the seventh commandment is "You shall not murder" (Ex. 20:13, NKJV). Life is a gift from God, and only He has the authority to bring it to a conclusion:

Today I have given you the choice between life and death, between blessings and curses. Now I call on heaven and earth to witness the choice you make. Oh, that you would choose life, so that you and your descendants might live! You can make this choice by loving the LORD your God, obeying him, and committing yourself firmly to him. This is the key to your life.
DEUTERONOMY 30:19-20, NLT

It is possible for a Christian to be chronically depressed. Many Christians suffer from a myriad of mental illnesses. If you are depressed, you are not alone. Just because people have received Jesus Christ as their Savior does not eradicate their behavioral weaknesses; their hereditary; or their biological, mental, and emotional state.

Read 1 Corinthians 6:19-20; 10:12-13. How these verses apply to suicide?

What warnings do these verses convey to you personally?

DO PEOPLE WHO COMMIT SUICIDE GO TO HELL?

Some people believe suicide is an unforgivable sin, but this is not a biblical teaching. God forgives all sin except the sin of rejecting Jesus Christ as Savior and Lord. The salvation we receive from Jesus Christ is eternal, regardless of our mental state or our spiritual maturity or immaturity. Paul the apostle wrote:

> In Him you also trusted, after you heard the word of truth, the gospel of your salvation; in whom also, having believed, you were sealed with the Holy Spirit of promise.
> **EPHESIANS 1:13, NKJV**

A seal in biblical times referred to a finished transaction, complete ownership. When we received Christ as Savior, we were, in a sense, locked in God's family by the substitutionary death Jesus Christ endured for us on the cross. In addition, the Holy Spirit indwelled us at the moment of our salvation, giving us the spiritual capacity to live a life above the power of sin:

> Sin shall not have dominion over you, for you are not under law but under grace.
> **ROMANS 6:14, NKJV**

Read the following passages and record what the Bible declares as true of those who have received Jesus Christ.

Mark 16:16

John 3:16-17

John 10:28

Romans 10:13

Ephesians 2:8

Based on these verses, how would you respond to someone who says a completed suicide is an unforgivable sin?

These verses make it clear that a genuine believer who commits suicide is not doomed to hell but is secure in the saving grace of Jesus Christ. There is no question, however, that for a believer to die by suicide is a poor testimony, regardless of the situation. God desires us to follow Him, and He promises to bless us with purpose and lasting fulfillment:

> He heals the brokenhearted
> and binds up their wounds.
> **PSALM 147:3, NIV**

> We are afflicted in every way, but not crushed;
> perplexed, but not despairing; persecuted, but
> not forsaken; struck down, but not destroyed.
> **2 CORINTHIANS 4:8-9, NASB**

Our Savior cries out to us:

> Come to me, all you who are weary
> and burdened, and I will give you rest.
> **MATTHEW 11:28, NIV**

What hope for people with suicidal tendencies is offered in these verses?

Yes, suicide happens, increasingly so, even among pastors and other Christians. We may not completely understand, and we may not always be able to answer the *why* question satisfactorily, but we must be prepared to respond with compassion and grace.

Close your time in prayer. Praise God as the Creator of all life. Pray for anyone you know who is depressed, is contemplating suicide, or has been affected by suicide. Open your heart to God. Are you struggling with depression? What worries or anxious thoughts do you have today? Confess them to the Lord, asking Him to encourage you and to keep you in His care.

DAY 5

HOW TO INTERVENE

Every time a person dies by suicide there is, as suicidologists teach, a contagion effect. When someone dies by suicide, it common for a spouse, father, mother, brother, sister, or friend to attempt or complete suicide. This cluster effect frequently occurs in high schools across the nation, where teens attempt suicide after a classmate has died by suicide. These are often referred to as chain-reaction or copycat suicides. Rarely is detailed publicity the case today, with the exception of well-known celebrities like comedian Robin Williams, who killed himself with the onset of Parkinson's disease.[20] Sensationalizing suicide can cause troubled individuals to mimic a suicide attempt.

Talking intelligently about suicide does not cause suicide, but it can prevent it. Failing to talk about it can have disastrous consequences. You may not be an expert, but your care and compassion are essential, so know the facts and the fallacies about suicide.

Mark your answer to each statement below.

True False

☐   ☐   Talking about suicide plants the idea in a depressed person's mind.

☐   ☐   People who talk about suicide usually do not follow through with it.

☐   ☐   Most suicides occur without warning.

☐   ☐   When depression lifts, suicide is no longer a concern.

☐   ☐   A suicidal person cannot be talked out of dying if he or she is intent on it.

☐   ☐   Only certain people are the suicidal type.

☐   ☐   Only insane people complete suicide.

☐   ☐   If a person has survived a suicide attempt, the likelihood of a second attempt is diminished.

☐   ☐   People who complete suicide have not sought medical help prior to the attempt.

☐   ☐   Suicide is a new phenomenon. No one in the Bible attempted or completed suicide.[21]

All of these statements are false, and yet many of them are common fallacies.

Which of these fallacies surprises you most? Why?

The Bible includes accounts of several completed suicides:

- Abimelech, Judges 9:54
- Samson, Judges 16:29-31
- Saul and his armor bearer, 1 Samuel 31:3-6
- Ahithophel, 2 Samuel 17:23
- Zimri, 1 Kings 16:18
- Judas, Matthew 27:5

Additionally, scores of people in the Bible were depressed to such an extent that they wanted to die (see 1 Kings 19:4; Jonah 4:3; 2 Cor. 1:8). Because suicide is not part of God's plan, it is always presented unfavorably in Scripture.

STEPS OF INTERVENTION

I learned about suicide and its far-reaching collateral damage when I was very young. Since the early 1980s my father, Dr. Jerry Johnston, after decades of speaking to hundreds of thousands of students and interacting personally with many of them, has been widely considered to be an expert on the suicide epidemic in North America. He wrote a popular book, *Why Suicide?* and has worked closely with suicidology experts and mental-health professionals. These experts have provided a unique perspective on intervention and coping with loss.

When someone close to you talks about suicide or exhibits signs of suicidal desires, you can respond by taking five specific action steps. This is a strategy of compassion, concern, and intervention.

STEP 1: CAREFULLY LISTEN AND OBSERVE THE PERSON. When someone is suicidal, do not dominate the conversation or preach at the wounded person. Emotions are raw when a person is suicidal. Think of how gently you would respond to someone who had a broken arm, wrist, or leg. Approach the person with the same care, calmness, and attentiveness. Ask the suicidal person to explain to you what is bothering them. Let them talk. Even though it may be difficult, remain calm, listen, and look the person in the eyes. When someone is suicidal, they frequently self-medicate by abusing drugs and/or alcohol. When a friend or a family member is dependent on drugs, they are communicating to you by their behavior, not just their words. Care enough not to allow their addiction to grow worse year after year. A suicidal individual is counting on you to go the extra mile by carefully observing them, listening to their words and actions, and loving them enough to intervene. Listen and keep listening.

STEP 2: IDENTIFY WITH THE HURTING PERSON. If you do not identify with the suicidal person, there is a much higher risk that you will lose them to suicide. Do not use guilt by suggesting that if they were closer with God, they would not have suicidal thoughts. That is a myth. A Christian who acts like a judgmental Pharisee overlooks the fact that statistically, most people have entertained a momentary or perhaps more prolonged thought of suicide under intense stress.

STEP 3: INITIATE A LOVING, CALCULATED RESPONSE, BEING VERY CAREFUL AND SENSITIVE. Ignoring the suicidal person is the worst possible scenario. Perhaps you were raised in a family that never addressed issues and always swept problems under the rug. That approach is dysfunctional. A healthy person seeks healing for a friend or a family member who is struggling with suicidal thoughts. Saving your family member or friend will require you to interrupt your normal schedule. That is OK. Remember that most people spell *love* t-i-m-e. Invest time in creating an action to bring the person out of the depth of their suicidal struggle.

STEP 4: ASK THE KEY QUESTION. Whenever you suspect that someone close to you is contemplating taking his or her life, an essential question must be asked: Do you have a plan or method to take your life? Have you considered an actual time to do it? If they have a plan, method, or timeline, they are in immediate danger. Stay with the hurting individual at all times. They should never be left alone. You must also commit to the time and expense of professional help. You do not need to lead the person to healing alone. Perhaps the person might need to be hospitalized. I always encourage a reputable Christian counselor and/or psychiatrist or a trained, experienced pastor to lead an intervention with specific healing steps.

STEP 5: ACCESS THE NATIONAL SUICIDE PREVENTION LIFELINE. "Like" the National Suicide Prevention Lifeline Facebook page: *www.facebook.com/ 800273TALK*. This phenomenal organization interfaces with Facebook to geographically pinpoint suicidal comments on Facebook and intervenes with responses to provide assistance. Or phone them at 800.273.TALK.

> Read engagement principle 4 in the box. Why is asking questions important when talking with someone about invisible illnesses?

How would you show compassion when talking with someone who is depressed or suicidal?

Imagine yourself talking with someone you love who is exhibiting signs of suicidal thoughts. Using the previous five steps, prayerfully outline your own strategy. Be as specific as you can. Record what you would do and not do, how you would approach the person, and what you would say.

Pray for anyone you know who is or might be exhibiting signs of suicidal thoughts. Pray for counselors who work with people who are in trouble. Ask God to give you wisdom and courage.

■ ENGAGEMENT PRINCIPLE 4

Be curious. Ask questions; allow the other person to be an "expert." Being smart does not mean you think others are stupid.

The best technique to use with anyone is to ask questions. People respond much better to questions than to assertions. Questions require something of the person to whom you are speaking. Questions are conversational and can be flattering. When we know a friend or a family member is struggling emotionally, we need to be extra curious and take an interest in them personally.

This engagement principle is a natural follow-up to engagement principle 1, "Shut up and listen." As you discuss any topic, especially sensitive subjects like suicide and mental illness,

begin from a humble and compassionate attitude, as Jesus did. Although He knew everything, He was humble and asked lots of questions.

This week's personal study has provided statistics to make you more aware of the issues in society. It has also presented helpful Scripture passages, as well as guidelines for talking with someone about these issues. While it is good to feel confident and comfortable in your knowledge of the topic, it is important that you do not appear arrogant or uncaring to the person with whom you are engaging. Stay attuned to the cry of their heart and respond with compassion.

PAIN TOLERANCE

WHY DO WE EXPERIENCE SUFFERING AND PAIN?

JOHN 19:29

that the Scripture might be fulfilled, He said, "I'm thirsty!" [29] A jar full of sour wine was sitting there; so they fixed a sponge full of sour wine on hyssop[a] and held it up to His mouth.
[a]Ps 69:21

[30] When Jesus had received the sour wine, He said, [a]"It is finished!" Then bowing His head, He [b]gave up His spirit.
[a]Jn 17:4 [b]Php 2:8

Jesus' Side Pierced

[31] Since it was the preparation day, the Jews [b]did not want the bodies to remain on the cross on the Sabbath (that Sabbath was [c]a special[b] day). requested that Pilate have their legs broken and that their bodies taken away. [32] So the soldiers and broke the legs of the first and of the other one who was crucified with Him. [33] When they came to Jesus, they did not break His legs, since they saw that He was already dead. [34] But one of the soldiers pierced His side with a spear, and at once blood and water came out. [35] He who saw this has testified so that you also may believe. His testimony is true, and he knows he is telling the truth. [36] For these things happened [e]so that the Scripture would be fulfilled: Not one of His bones will be broken. [37] Also, another Scripture says: [g]They will look at the One they pierced.[d]
[a]Mk 15:42 [b]Dt 21:23 [c]Ex 12:16 [d]Zch 13:1 [e]Jn 20:31; 1Jn 1:1 [f]Ex 12:46; Ps 34:20 [g]Zch 12:10

Jesus' Burial

who was a disciple of Jesus—but secretly [a]because of his fear of the Jews—asked Pilate that he might remove Jesus' body. Pilate gave him permission, so he came and took His body away. [39] Nicodemus (who had previously come to Him at night) also came, bringing a mixture of about 75 pounds[e] of myrrh and aloes. [40] Then they took Jesus' body and wrapped it in linen cloths with the aromatic spices, according to the burial custom of the Jews. [41] There was a garden in the place where He was crucified. A [d]new tomb was in the garden; no one had yet been placed in it. [42] [e]They placed Jesus there because of the Jewish preparation and since the tomb was nearby.
[a]Mt 27:57 [b]Pr 29:25 [c]Jn 3:1-2 [d]Mt 27:60; Lk 23:53 [e]Is 53:9

The Empty Tomb

20 On the [a]first day of the week, Mary Magdalene came to the tomb early, while it was still dark. She saw that the stone had been removed from the tomb. [2] So she ran to Simon Peter and to the other disciple, the one Jesus loved, and said to them, "They have taken the Lord out of the tomb, and we don't know where they have put Him!" [3] At that Peter and the other disciple went out, heading for the tomb. [4] The two were running together, but the other disciple outran Peter and got to the tomb first. [5] Stooping down, he saw [b]the linen cloths lying there, yet he did not go in. [6] Then, following him, Simon Peter came also. He entered the tomb and saw the linen cloths lying there. [7] The wrapping that had been on His head was not lying with the linen cloths but was folded up in a separate place by itself. [8] The other disciple, who had reached the tomb first, then entered the tomb, saw, and believed. [9] For they still did not understand the [c]Scripture that He must rise from the dead. [10] Then the disciples went home again.

START

Steve Jobs was one of the most iconic people of our time. His innovations have shaped and connected the world. No wonder he appeared on the cover of *Time* eight times between 1982 and 2011. Earlier in life Steve Jobs had an unanswered question that, tragically, caused him to walk away from his Christian faith. Walter Isaacson wrote these chilling words about Jobs's loss of faith at 13 years of age:

> In July 1968 *Life* magazine published a shocking cover showing a pair of starving children in Biafra. Jobs took it to Sunday school and confronted the church's pastor. "If I raise my finger, will God know which one I'm going to raise even before I do it?" The pastor answered, "Yes, God knows everything." Jobs then pulled out the *Life* cover and asked, "Well, does God know about this and what's going to happen to those children?" "Steve, I know you don't understand, but yes, God knows about that." Jobs announced that he didn't want to have anything to do with worshipping such a God, and he never went back to church.[1]

What questions have you had about the existence of evil and suffering in the world?

Perhaps the most prevalent unanswered question people have today is the question of tragedy, pain, and suffering. As Christian thinkers, we must be prepared to answer these questions for the young Steve Jobses of the world.

Have your questions about evil and suffering ever led you to question your faith in God, as Jobs did? If so, could you briefly share that part of your faith journey?

How do we answer the unanswered questions of suffering in our own minds, as well as those of our family, friends, and coworkers? Let's see what Jeremiah has to teach us today.

WATCH

1. I can and should be honest about the reality of my suffering and pain.

2. I come to know God better through my pain and suffering.

3. My response to suffering determines my future.

4. I do not suffer in vain. God's plan and blessings are not canceled by my trials.

RESPOND

What one truth from Jeremiah's teaching resonated most with you?

How is it possible that we live in a world that requires cancer wards for precious little children plagued with terminal illnesses? Suffering and evil are no respecter of age, reputation, or social status, and unfortunately, tragedies occur with regularity. For all of our cultural advances and sophistication, human trafficking, abuse, war, disease, slavery, and natural disasters relentlessly plague society.

How would you respond or how have you responded to the question of pain and suffering in the world to someone who has asked?

The Bible is replete with people who, like many of us, asked similar questions. Some demanded an answer from God. Job, David, Gideon, Jeremiah, Isaiah, John the Baptist, and even Jesus questioned God. The Bible has the integrity to be uncensored. It does not avoid the question of evil, suffering, and pain. Instead, we get a front-row seat to confrontations about this subject.

Read Judges 6:1-14.

What were the Israelites' lives like during the period described in verses 1-6?

What purposes did this prophet's reminder from the past serve?

In view of all the tragedy around him, Gideon had the audacity to interrupt the angel who was bringing him a direct word from God. Gideon had a burning unanswered question for the messenger from God:

> "Pardon me, my lord," Gideon replied, "but if the LORD is with us, why has all this happened to us?"
>
> **JUDGES 6:13, NIV**

When have you asked a "Why is this happening, God?" type of question? What were your circumstances?

What facts was Gideon overlooking when he asked his questions?

Notice that the angel of God did not chastise Gideon for his questions. Instead, the Lord gave him a mission; he put Gideon in a position to partner with God and become a solution to the Israelites' problems. God often uses the weak things of this world so that He receives glory (see 1 Cor. 1:27-29).

What lessons do you learn from this passage about God's perspective on evil and suffering?

In this week's individual study, we will examine the question of evil and suffering more closely. By the end you should be able to answer why suffering exists, what we should think about it, what God's ultimate purpose for us through suffering, and how we can find love and grace in the middle of it.

PRAY

- Close this final session by thanking God for His Word, His presence with you, and His sovereignty over all of life's circumstances.
- Ask Him to empower you as you engage with people whom He is already drawing to Himself.
- Thank God for bringing this group together to explore biblical answers to some of life's most difficult questions.

Read week 6 and complete the activities on the following pages to conclude this Bible study.

DAY 1

WHY IS THERE EVIL IN THE WORLD?

Suffering is the wake-up call you did not ask for and the nightmare that quickly becomes reality. Suffering, in rapid speed, can take you back to being five years old again and experiencing the utter terror of riding a bike for the first time without training wheels. Are you going to pedal, steer, and maneuver through this challenge in life without taking a massive tumble?

Suffering is like a mirror that reveals who we really are. Sometimes it's hard to recognize ourselves in the midst of trials. Suffering is elusive, even mysterious, often surfacing at the wrong time, in the wrong places, and with the wrong people. Suffering is a noun and a verb and a full stop altogether. Suffering is both self-explanatory and unexplainable. Suffering is a problem we all face at one time or another. Suffering cannot be unfriended; it is personal, local, regional, and long distance. Suffering is the most common human experience, and it will change most of us forever.

Suffering is an eternal unanswered question the Bible has an answer for and, with the correct theology, can be viewed as an incredible opportunity. So what is it about suffering that stops us in our tracks and almost paralyzes us with panic? Is it that we are weak, needy, and terrified of pain? Or could it be that deep down inside we wonder whether God will truly make good on His promise to be there for us (see Heb. 13:5)? C. S. Lewis revealed pertinent insight when asked about pain and suffering:

> We are not necessarily doubting that God will do the best for us;
> we are wondering how painful the best will turn out to be.[2]

In what ways have pain and suffering affected or changed you?

In this week's study we will answer three burning questions:

1. What is the problem of evil?
2. Why do evil, suffering, and pain exist?
3. How do we respond to the tragedies of life?

Some people believe the Bible does not provide an answer for the problem of evil. But in fact, Scripture addresses this serious question. It explains why there are evil, suffering, injustice, and tragedy in the world and how we can experience the peace of God through the trials of life.

Read Job 1. List evidence for evil and suffering you find in this passage.

From this passage, what is at least one explanation for evil and suffering?

The number one reason people walk away from faith is the personal experience of unexpected tragedy. I have considered and taught extensively on the problem of suffering; however, when my wife was rushed to the hospital after complications in childbirth and was given an emergency blood transfusion, suffering took on a new form, evolving from an intellectual question to a very personal problem. Therefore, if we have not prepared for suffering in our lives by answering the unanswered question of suffering, when the problems happen, we are unprepared to live through them.

When we consider the existence of evil and suffering in our world, there are actually two problems that must be addressed. The first problem is one of perception: the problem of a good God and the reality of evil. The second is the experiential problem that asks, "How do I survive my personal suffering and the pain in the world around me?" Suffering and pain hit us from all sides: mentally, spiritually, emotionally, and physically. The good news is that there are biblical answers for both of these particular problems.

While the perceptive approach might be interesting to discuss and debate in a more detached discussion in Bible study, the experiential issue requires pastoral care and an encouraging presence. Consider Job and his friends. Job could have used more sympathy and silence instead of false accusations and attempted explanations from his friends. My friend Pastor Greg Laurie and I happened to be in Jerusalem at the same time leading tours of the Holy Land two years after he tragically lost his 33-year-old son, Christopher. Spending time with Greg was a moving experience because he transparently and inspirationally shared how he and Cathe were living through this tragedy by the grace of God. One of the best sermons I have ever heard was when Greg shared what not to say to someone who is grieving, such as "I know what you are going through." We really do not know. Making the wrong comment to a grieving friend or family member can worsen the suffering. We learn similar lessons when we study the Book of Job.

Read Job 11:7-15.

If you were this friend of suffering Job, what would you do to be an encouraging presence to him rather than trying to provide a reasoned theological argument?

In *The Problem of Pain* C. S. Lewis argued that he had nothing to offer ...

> ... except my conviction that when pain is to be borne, a little courage helps more than much knowledge, a little human sympathy more than much courage, and the least extract of the love of God more than all.[3]

Our young son once had a major kidney operation that required a hospital stay for several nights. Watching a child suffer can make it difficult for some people to believe in God. Experiencing our two-year-old son suffer through the recovery process clouded our intellectual answers for why this was happening. Rather, our emotional need totally eclipsed our intellectual need for answers.

A good friend of mine—one of the kindest, most morally upright people I know—is an atheist because a four year-old child died in his arms. Did God do that? Why would God allow such a tragedy? The amount of excruciating pain, unexplainable problems, and global suffering is so prevalent that some people have great difficulty believing in God or having any faith at all. We have a choice as Christian thinkers: to write those people off because of their disbelief or to compassionately, prayerfully help them find answers. If I have not experienced a crisis in my life, I should expect one. Therefore, I should be prepared for that coming problem spiritually, emotionally, physically, and mentally by maintaining a Jesus-centric view of the problem of evil, suffering, and pain.

Close today's study in prayer. Recognize the presence of Jesus as you begin. Simply tell Him what is on your heart right now. This might involve personal suffering or pain, the troubles of someone you love, or something going on in the world. Pray for people who are far away from God, especially if suffering is a barrier to belief for them.

DAY 2

DIGGING DEEPER

In October 1871 the great Chicago fire reduced significant portions of the city to ashes. D. L. Moody was preaching the Sunday evening when the inferno began to spread and did not know whether his children had survived until 24 hours later. Emma Moody later recalled that her mother's hair began turning gray that night when she was overcome with worry and anxiety at the thought of the inferno taking her children. Little did Mrs. Moody know that her dear friends, the Spaffords, had saved her children from the fire and had taken them into their home in Buena Park. This was the same Spafford family who only a few years later would suffer the loss of their four little girls in the sinking of the Ville de Havre in the mid-Atlantic. Moody biographer Kevin Belmonte tells the rest of the story:

> Sometimes history converges in unforgettable ways. The terrible sea disaster became the inspiration for Horatio Spafford to share his enduring faith by writing, "It Is Well with my Soul," the now classic hymn. It staggers the imagination to think that the Spaffords were able to help save the Moody children but would later suffer the loss of their own four daughters.[4]

I will never forget standing in the Mamertine prison in Rome, where tradition says Paul spent his last days. Similar to a dungeon, it was Rome's version of death row. I thought of how Paul's strength through God empowered him to face suffering, knowing that the end was near. In the very room I was standing Paul wrote:

> For this reason I also suffer these things, but I am
> not ashamed; for I know whom I have believed
> and I am convinced that He is able to guard
> what I have entrusted to Him until that day.
> **2 TIMOTHY 1:12, NASB**

Only God can enable us to see our trials as temporary experiences, as awful as they may be, and as preparation for the exceeding joy and glory of His eternal presence. The apostle Paul said that our present suffering is a "momentary, light affliction" that will last only a short time and that it prepares us for the glory of heaven (2 Cor. 4:17-18, NASB). From his prison cell Paul wrote to the persecuted church at Philippi, admonishing it to "rejoice in the Lord always" (Phil. 4:4, NASB).

Isaiah 26:3 reminds us:

> You keep him in perfect peace
> whose mind is stayed on you,
> because he trusts in you.
> **ISAIAH 26:3, ESV**

We serve a God who promises us that one day "He will wipe away every tear from [our] eyes" (Rev. 21:4, ESV).

In what specific ways do these promises from God's Word bring you comfort today?

God, through His Son and now through His Spirit, has entered our world of suffering. In the midst of our trials, He offers His presence, peace, hope, joy, and eternal life.

SIN IS EVER-PRESENT IN OUR WORLD

The Christian doctrine most confirmed by everyday experience is that humans are sinful and fallen. The fall of humanity had a comprehensive effect. God created man and women without sin and described His creation as "very good" (Gen. 1:31, ESV). Unlike any of the other created wonders, men and women were made in God's image (see v. 27). Nonetheless, Adam and Eve decided they knew better than God, and their choice introduced sin into the world and separated humanity from God (see Gen. 3).

Read Romans 5:12. What did the original sin bring into the world?

How have you witnessed personal loss and suffering as the result of sin?

IS OUR SUFFERING ALWAYS BECAUSE OF SIN?

Not all suffering in individual experiences is necessarily related to any specific disobedience. Jesus made that clear in the case of the blind man at the pool of Siloam (see John 9:1-3). All suffering came about because of sin introduced in general through the fall, but not all suffering is caused by personal sin.

Read Hebrews 12:5-11. Can you identify a time when God lovingly yet sternly disciplined you as His child? If so, what did you learn, and how did you grow through that experience?

Conclude today's study in prayer, thanking your Father for His discipline, as well as for His presence with you, His peace that rises above your circumstances (see Phil. 4:7), the hope and joy you have in Christ, and the eternal life He has provided for you.

DAY 3

THE EXISTENCE OF GRACE AND LOVE

[God] makes his sun rise on the evil and on the good,
and sends rain on the just and on the unjust.
MATTHEW 5:45, ESV

In day 1 we stated that the problem of evil, suffering, and pain is the number one reason people walk away from belief in God. Many find it hard to reconcile the presence of evil and the presence of a caring God. Does God really love me if He allows me to experience tragedy? An atheist friend once asked me, "If God exists, why does He not show up and visit a children's hospital?" Do you know what my answer is? God does show up through His church.

How do we respond to this line of thinking? All belief systems—not only Christianity but also atheism, Hinduism, no religious preference, Islam, agnosticism, cults, secular philosophies, and so on—must attempt to answer the problem of suffering.[5] In Christianity we find the best answer—the only answer—for the unanswered questions of evil, suffering, and pain.

While you are answering the problem of evil, you must answer the existence of grace as well. Why are there so many wonderful things in the world? Why do we love? The message of Christianity explains why there are grace, beauty, love peace, and goodwill. The message of the cross inspires many who, in the face of great adversity, sacrifice, care, love, go to extreme measures for noble purposes. Christianity makes sense of why people try to behave well and do the right thing. From the earliest days of the Christian movement, believers have taught and believed "God so loved the world" (John 3:16, NKJV); that is, God loved all people, created in His image. In contrast, Islam teaches that Allah does not love non-Muslims (see the Koran 3:32; 22:38; 30:45).[6]

How does your worldview affect the way you personally make sense of evil, suffering, and pain?

Let's look at ways Jesus addressed the problem of evil.

Read Luke 13:1-5.

Because unexpected tragedies occur in our world and since all of us are sinners, how should we respond to these tragedies?

List specific examples of beauty, grace, and love you have experienced.

In 2015 the Christian Thinkers Society filmed interviews at the national American Atheism Convention. We asked many of the atheists the *why* question: "Why did you become an atheist?" Two reasons were offered in nearly every interview: suffering in the world and the lack of critical thinking. The world is not as it ought to be, most of the atheists said. Think about that response. It implies a standard of objective, worldwide virtue, grace, and goodness. According to atheists, when we are dead, there is nothing—no afterlife, no postmortem existence. Life is a cosmic accident and has no value. However, if there are no God and no afterlife, and the material world (what we can experience with our five senses) is all that exists, why would we expect anything good in our lives now?

If atheists appeal to evil to argue against God, how are they in a position to judge something as evil or wrong? With no absolutes how can we judge what is right or wrong, good or bad? Compared to what? It is impossible to differentiate evil from good unless there is an absolute standard for how things "ought to be."[7] The very fact that we observe right versus wrong, good versus evil, suffering versus blessing argues for the image of God that is inherent in our souls.

C. S. Lewis wrote:

> My argument against God was that the universe seemed so cruel and unjust. But how had I got this idea of just and unjust? A man does not call a line crooked unless he has some idea of a straight line. What was I comparing this universe with when I called it unjust? If the whole show was bad and senseless from A to Z, so to speak, why did I, who was supposed to be part of the show, find myself in such violent reaction against it? … Thus in the very act of trying to prove that God did not exist—in other words, that the whole of reality was senseless—I found I was forced to assume that one part of reality—namely my idea of justice—was full of sense. Consequently atheism turns out to be too simple. If the whole universe has no meaning, we should never have found out that it has no meaning: just as, if there were no light in the universe and therefore no creatures with eyes, we should never know it was dark. Dark would be without meaning.[8]

Take a look at Paul's transparency about his own suffering:

> We do not want you to be uninformed, brothers and sisters, about the troubles we experienced in the province of Asia. We were under great pressure, far beyond our ability to endure, so that we despaired of life itself.
> **2 CORINTHIANS 1:8, NIV**

■ BIBLICAL TRUTHS TO REMEMBER WHEN YOU SUFFER

1. Every trial you face is allowed by God for your ultimate good (see Rom. 8:28-30; Heb. 12:5-11).
2. Your trial does not need to steal your joy (see 2 Cor. 12:9-10; 1 Pet. 4:12-14).
3. God is never more present than when you are suffering (see Ps. 34:18; Jas. 4:8).
4. Until you embrace your trial in unwavering submission to God, you will not reap the good (see Matt. 26:42; Jas. 1:2-5).[9]

When did Christianity get reduced to being cheery and happy all the time? In 2 Corinthians 1:8 Paul was honest and transparent about the problems, pain, suffering, and evil he encountered in his life and ministry. Paul's opponents had actually declared that Paul was not an apostle because he had so many problems, and it seemed God had abandoned him. Paul, on the other hand, argued that his suffering was in fact the very mark of his apostleship (see 3:1-18). In 4:1 Paul declared, "We do not lose heart" (NIV), even though his reality was one of brokenness and suffering: "afflicted in every way, but not crushed" (v. 8, NIV).

God permits or allows suffering, but He never causes it. God sees the end from the beginning. We are free to choose. We are not robots. God permits us to make bad, life-ruining decisions; however, in His sovereignty and control, permitting us to make freewill decisions, God ultimately causes His good purposes to be achieved, even through the sinful choices people make (see Gen. 50:20; Rom 8:28).

The perfect example is the atoning, substitutionary death of Jesus Christ. Jesus experienced injustice and evil at "the hands of lawless men" (Acts 2:23, ESV); however, God's ultimate purpose for redemption transcended the atrocity of killing the only perfect person who ever lived. Many of us can look back at difficult situations we have experienced and admit that God ultimately brought good from a difficult situation.

Read 2 Corinthians 12:7b-10.

What does Paul's explanation about the cause of his pain tell you about the source of evil and suffering?

Consider an area in which you have suffered or are suffering. In what ways can God's grace be sufficient for you? In what specific ways can you boast in your weakness?

The question of evil appears to be eternal, but in fact, evil had a beginning, and it will have an end. According to the teachings of the Bible, evil is not eternal. As we reflect on the problems of evil, we must also consider the existence of grace and love. They are clear evidence that in spite of the reality of evil and suffering, God sustains, strengthens, and blesses His children.

As you close in prayer, take inventory of all the grace God has shown you and praise Him for all the love He extends to you that you do not deserve. Use this psalm to thank God for His goodness:

> Praise the LORD.
> Give thanks to the LORD, for he is good;
>   his love endures forever.
> **PSALM 106:1, NIV**

DAY 4

HOW DO WE VIEW SUFFERING?

In the midwest region of America known as Tornado Alley, tornado drills, sirens on the first Wednesday of every month, tornado shelters, watches, and warnings are part of the fabric of life. Despite all this preparation, most casualties are often the result of unpreparedness. The same is true for Christians. The Bible has many storm warnings about life and hardship.

Sadly, some people reveal their Christian immaturity when they suffer. Many Christians in the West have embraced a theology that rests on the fallacy that nothing bad can happen to you after you become a Christian. So when trials, tests, and tragedies come—and make no mistake; they will—those problems undermine their faith, a faith that was based on circumstances in this life.

Authentic Christian faith is never surprised by adversity and problems. Randy Alcorn wisely wrote in *If God is Good*, "The faith that can't be shaken is the faith that has been shaken."[10] God is faithful. Our faith is refined when we suffer, because we learn by experience that God is good and trustworthy:

> Behold, I have refined you, but not as silver;
> I have tried you in the furnace of affliction.
> **ISAIAH 48:10, ESV**

What is your reaction to this verse? What does the idea of refinement mean here? What is it we are being refined for?

The ultimate purpose of life is not our happiness but rather a relationship with Jesus Christ. Who is this God who has made innumerable promises to us in His Word? Shouldn't we get to know Him?

Do you believe in a concierge God? Is God your personal concierge from heaven? One reason the problem of evil has so much traction is that many Western Christians assume that if God exists, then His purpose for our lives is our personal comfort and happiness—because it's all about us. Unfortunately, much popular preaching in American churches is based on a theology that says God's role is to create a comfortable environment for His human favorites.

We will be perplexed in our suffering if we have the mindset that being a Christian means we will never suffer. A biblical worldview, in contrast, asserts that God is not a cosmic concierge service and that the primary purpose of human life is not happiness. Our purpose is to know God, make Him known, glorify Him, and proclaim His plan for salvation to the world. God created us with a purpose.

We come to know God better in our trials. When the New Testament addresses the problems of evil, suffering, and tragedy, the emphasis is not on the cause of the suffering, nor is it on a miraculous escape from suffering. Instead, the New Testament affirms the presence of Jesus in the crisis, what we can learn, who we become, and how we should respond.

How have you come to know God better through suffering or painful circumstances?

What does each of the following Bible verses reveal to you about the reason, goal, or purpose of suffering?

Job 19:25-27

Acts 16:25-29

2 Corinthians 4:16-18

Philippians 1:29

My wife and I have visited some of the most lethal places on earth for Christians. Our interaction with Chinese Christians who are courageous enough to survive; forgive; love; and most of all, believe amid atheist aggression has been life-changing. In some of the countries where Christians experience the most intense suffering, the church is expanding exponentially. What was true in the Book of Acts is true today: there is a symbiotic relationship between suffering and growth rates of Christianity in the world. The more the church is persecuted, the more the church is made uncomfortable, and the more the church and its mission expand. As a modern example, consider that there are now more Christians than Communists in China. Recent surveys calculate the number of mainland Christians worshiping independently of the state churches to be as high as one hundred million. Nearly 1 in 10 Chinese people is a Christian. There are now more Chinese Christians than American Christians.[11]

> Where sin abounded, grace abounded much more.
> **ROMANS 5:20, NKJV**

This verse has been a guidepost in my life when I have faced trials. In Greek this passage promises a superabounding *(huperperisseúo)*, or lavish, grace. You can experience God's lavish grace too. God supplies superabounding grace for all of us to withstand the suffering we experience in our lives. When Christians suffer, we have a confident expectation: God is in total control.

Read Romans 8:28-32. How do these verses summarize the Christian worldview toward suffering and evil?

■ A WORD STUDY OF ROMANS 8:28

"KNOW"—to know something "intuitively or instinctively,"[10] though we may not fully understand or sense it experientially.

"WHO LOVE GOD"—to us who love God, He promises to work all things together for good.

"ALL THINGS"—God cannot forget and will not overlook any experience in our lives.

"WORK TOGETHER"—similar to our English word *synergize*. God continually partners with us in our suffering.

"FOR GOOD"—God can turn every experience for our good and His glory.

"HIS PURPOSE"—God's plan and purpose for our lives. The emphasis is on God's plan, not ours.

Verses 31-32 remind us that God is for us even in the midst of great suffering. He suffers with us. As followers of Jesus, we can have assurance that the same God …

> … who did not spare his own Son but gave him up for us all, how will he not also with him graciously give us all things?
> **ROMANS 8:32, ESV**

God is controlling the momentary circumstances of our lives. He is in total control (see Rom. 8:28).

Read Ephesians 1:15-23.

The focus of Paul's prayer life for himself and the dominant element in his intercession for the churches he started were always to know God better (see v. 17). Paul never prayed for life to get easier or more comfortable; rather, he said, "I have learned to be content whatever the circumstances" (Phil. 4:11, NIV). The more I know God, the more I come to understand that He knows me. Knowing God is the goal—the apex—of the Christian life. If we are to transcend the tragedies of life, we must learn to experientially know God better and thereby embody the kind of faith that sustains us in the challenging days ahead.

Similar to the way Paul prayed in Ephesians 1, Jeremiah preached:

> Let not a wise man boast of his wisdom, and let not the mighty man boast of his might, let not a rich man boast of his riches; but let him who boasts boast of this, that he understands and knows Me, that I am the LORD who exercises lovingkindness, justice and righteousness on earth.
> **JEREMIAH 9:23-24, NASB**

Keep your Bible open to Ephesians 1:15-23 and use it as a model for your personal prayer today. Ask God to help you know Him better, through both good and painful life circumstances. Thank God that He is sovereign, in complete control. Praise Him for his incomparably great power.

DAY 5

WHAT IS GOD'S ULTIMATE PURPOSE FOR SUFFERING?

Charles Spurgeon ministered from the pain of intense personal suffering through gout and related diseases. His wife was an invalid confined to her room during 10 of the most productive years of his ministry. On one particularly difficult evening, Spurgeon visited his wife's room. As he sat gazing into the crackling fire, he listened to the symphony of sounds echoing in the vacuous room. As a fire burns, it consumes and decomposes the wood into several forms of gas (smoke), char, and ash, which, for Spurgeon, produced a swift musical tone. Pulling himself up by his bootstraps, Spurgeon whispered to his wife, "Susannah, it takes the fire to bring out the music."[12]

> **Reflect on Spurgeon's statement. In what ways or circumstances have you found that to be true?**

On this last day of individual study, we will look at four principles that affirm God's ultimate power over and purpose for evil and suffering.

1. GOD ALLOWS AND IS IN CONTROL OF ALL MY CHALLENGES

In Genesis 39 God allowed Joseph to be wrongfully accused by Potiphar's wife and then thrown into prison, where he waited 13 years before he finally had an audience with Pharaoh. Was Joseph right with God? Was he living obediently? Yes. And yet God allowed this problem to occur because He had an ultimate purpose in mind. After his trial was over, Joseph could says to his brothers, "You meant evil against me, but God meant it for good" (Gen. 50:20).

How do you see this principle in action in your life? That challenge in your life that you think is trying to destroy you—God is using it for good. God wants to get you to a place in your Christian life where you are utterly dependent on Him. Those experiences in Joseph's life that were meant for evil were actually a disguised blessing. God had a much greater purpose not only in Joseph's life but also for all of Israel. Through Joseph's rise to power and wise leadership, the messianic line of Abraham was saved from famine.

As you look back on the problems and challenges of your life,
when did a problem turn out to be a disguised blessing?

2. I MUST TAKE RESPONSIBILITY FOR WHAT I CAN DO AND ALLOW GOD TO DO THE SUPERNATURAL

Believers in Jesus grossly misinterpret the sovereignty of God when they make the following statements.

- "If God wants me out of this problem, He will get me out of it; I don't need to do anything."
- "If God wants that family member reached, He will reach them; He doesn't need me to say anything."
- "If God wants me to build this ministry, I need to sit back and wait for it to grow."

These are misguided excuses not to act responsibly. In the Bible God always chose to work through human agency. For example, when God asked the prophet Isaiah, "Who will go for us?" Isaiah spoke right up and said, "Here I am! Send me" (Isa. 6:8, ESV).

When believers go through challenges, they need to be ready to pray, "Lord, here I am. Show me what You want me to do. Open the doors You want me to walk through. It is time for things to change."

Often the issue is not so much a struggle with evil as the need for a personal decision: Will I trust the Lord in hard times? Shadrach, Meshach, and Abednego would rather have died trusting God than live outside His plan. They had no guarantees that God would physically protect them from the fiery furnace, and yet they uttered three of the most courageous words in the Bible—"But if not":

> If this be so, our God whom we serve is able to deliver
> us from the burning fiery furnace, and he will deliver
> us out of your hand, O king. But if not, be it known
> to you, O king, that we will not serve your gods or
> worship the golden image that you have set up.
> **DANIEL 3:17-18, ESV**

Will you make the decision to trust the fact that God is in control, no matter what challenges you face? Even if you are not facing a challenge right now, it is an important act of faith to make this decision before you face one. Record your affirmation of trust below.

3. SUFFERING CAN CONFIRM MY FAITH

When we suffer, we realize how insignificant our lives are apart from living them in the will of God. We see that the real value of life is not in the temporal realm but in eternal matters. Abraham proved his faith by his willingness to sacrifice his son of promise, Isaac (see Gen. 22). Like Abraham, we must make the decision to persevere in our faith. Let us also never forget that just as God provided the ram in Abraham's story, God is bringing our solution in His perfect timing.

Read James 1:2-5.

How have you seen trials develop perseverance and maturity in your life?

■ COME FORTH AS GOLD

The refining process of gold vividly depicts God's purposes behind trials. When gold ore comes out of the ground, it is mixed with other metals and impurities. To be refined, gold must first be melted, so it is placed in furnaces and heated to 1,010 degrees Celsius.

The second refiner's step is binding. Once the gold is molten, it is mixed with a special flux to make it more fluid and to bind the impurities together. Then, when the gold is poured into a mold, the impurities, called slag, rise to the top.

Finally, the gold is separated. After it has cooled, the slag is broken off. Then the steps are repeated, sometimes multiple times for greater purity.

That's what Job had in mind when he said: "He knows the way that I take; When he has tried me, I shall come out as gold," Job 23:10, ESV.

Although Job questioned the reason behind God's methods, He never rebelled against God.

Your trial is refining you. Can you feel the heat? Can you see the slag rising to the surface? Some people go into the furnace of affliction and get burned; others go in and get purified. If you submit to the Lord, as painful as the crisis may be, it will refine you and make you better. If you resist what God is doing, the furnace will only burn. If this trial is making your faith purer and stronger and you're not bitter toward the Lord and you're learning to love and trust Him more, you are coming out as gold.[13]

It is not *if* but *when* we face various trials. Believers who expect their Christian lives to be easy are in for a shock. Jesus warned His disciples:

> In the world you will have tribulation.
> But take heart; I have overcome the world.
> **JOHN 16:33, ESV**

4. SOMEDAY EVERYTHING WILL BECOME CLEAR, AND GOD'S ULTIMATE PURPOSE WILL BE ACCOMPLISHED

Biblical heroes like Abraham, Joseph, Job, and others did not have clarity about their trials in the midst of them. It was only later that they realized what God was doing during the crisis. Job's beloved wife, perhaps fatigued and frustrated after watching her husband suffer in agony, encouraged him to "curse God and die" (Job 2:9, ESV). Israel's greatest warrior even felt abandoned by God, asking Him, "Why have you forsaken me?" (Ps. 22: 1, ESV). Habakkuk was overwhelmed with the question *why*. There was evil in Judah. God was even using the evil Babylonians as the instrument of correction for His own people. God told Habakkuk what we all need to hear during times of suffering: "The just shall live by his faith" (2:4, NKJV).

Even Jesus suffered depression and such sorrow prior to His crucifixion that He nearly died (see Matt. 26:38). So intense was His pain that He asked His Father, "If it is possible, let this cup pass from Me" (Matt 26:39, NASB). Only a few hours later He would sense such unimaginable abandonment from His Father that He would cry out, "My God, my God, why have you forsaken me?" (Matt. 27:46, ESV). The author of Hebrews recorded these profound thoughts for us:

> We do not have a high priest who is unable to empathize
> with our weaknesses, but we have one who has been
> tempted in every way, just as we are—yet he did not sin.
> **HEBREWS 4:15, NIV**

> Never will I leave you;
> never will I forsake you.
> **HEBREWS 13:5, NIV**

Jesus persevered through His suffering in obedience to His Father. Through His experience we can be confident that He knows what we are going through when we suffer and that God will bring about His good purposes for our lives as He brought victory over evil through Jesus.

Read engagement principle 5 and think of a question you have heard about why evil and suffering exist. How do those questions tend to come up?

When you are asked a tough question about God in the face of evil and suffering, what are some ways you can make truth attractive?

Close your time in prayer. Praise your all-powerful, ever-present God. Confess to Him times when you have failed to trust Him and instead have relied on your own power. Pray for wisdom as you engage with people God puts in your path who need the anchor of a belief system rooted in the person of Jesus Christ and in the truth of His Word.

◼ ENGAGEMENT PRINCIPLE 5

Don't go beast mode.

Learn how to answer tough questions in a winsome way as a thoughtful ambassador for Christ. Often the way we respond to someone's questions is as important as, or perhaps even more important than, what we say. We need to learn how to answer tough questions in a winsome way as thoughtful ambassadors for Christ. Titus 2:10 by states that believers should "make the teaching about God our Savior attractive in every way" (NLT). Paul used the word *kosméo*, which is similar to our English word *cosmetics* or *decorate*. In telling believers to make the gospel attractive, Paul was saying the way we act decorates the gospel and makes it more engaging to the world around us. Your concern for communicating the gospel must always outweigh your impulse to go beast mode. You can start by saying, "That is a great question."

Philosophical questions about the relationship between suffering and a good, all-powerful God can be challenging. Be up-front about the difficulty of the topic. Humbly say, "I am not so arrogant to think I have all the answers, but I know the Bible says …" Even if we do not always have all the right words, we always have the Holy Spirit to guide us. We also have the joy of Christ in us, joy that can be attractive and contagious.

NOTES

WEEK 1

1. Catherine Soanes and Angus Stevenson, eds., *Concise Oxford English Dictionary* (Oxford: Oxford University Press, 2004).
2. Henry and Richard Blackaby and Claude King, *Experiencing God* Bible study (Nashville: LifeWay, 2007), 115.
3. Ibid., 116.
4. Ibid., 121.
5. Ibid., 122.
6. Ibid., 120.
7. Ludwig Koehler, Walter Baumgartner, and Johann Jakob Stamm, trans. M. E. J. Richardson, *The Hebrew and Aramaic Lexicon of the Old Testament*, vol. 1 (Leiden, Netherlands: Brill Academic Publishers, 1999).

WEEK 2

1. April 7, A.D. 33, is an alternative date for the crucifixion of Jesus. For a more detailed analysis of the dating of Jesus' death and resurrection, see Robert H. Stein, *Jesus the Messiah: A Survey of the Life of Christ* (Downers Grove, IL: InterVarsity Press, 1996), 39.
2. N. T. Wright, *The Resurrection of the Son of God: Christian Origins and the Question of God* (London: SPCK, 2003), 35.
3. Carol McPhall, "Easter Sunday Is the Super Bowl of Church Attendance," *AL.com* [online], 28 March 2013 [cited 3 September 2015]. Available from the Internet: *www.al.com/living/index.ssf/2013/03/easter_ranks_first_in_church_a.html*.
4. Bill Cook, "Resurrection of Jesus the Christ," *Holman Illustrated Bible Dictionary* (Nashville: Holman Bible Publishers, 2003), 1382.
5. Soanes, Catherine, and Angus Stevenson, eds. *Concise Oxford English Dictionary* (Oxford: Oxford University Press), 2004.
6. Preben Vang and Terry Carter, *Telling God's Story* (Nashville: B&H Publishing, 2006), 247.
7. James D. G. Dunn, *Jesus Remembered. Christianity in the Making*, vol. 1 (Grand Rapids: Eerdmans, 2003), 855.
8. Gary R. Habermas, *The Historical Jesus: Ancient Evidence for the Life of Christ* (Joplin: College Press, 1996), 153. See n. 44, which lists the scholars.
9. For more on this important topic, see Samuele Bacchiocchi, *From Sabbath to Sunday: A Historical Investigation of the Rise of Sunday Observance in Early Christianity* (Rome: The Pontifical Gregorian University Press, 1977).
10. N. T. Wright, "Paul, Arabia, and Elijah (Galatians 1:17)," *Journal of Biblical Literature* 115: 683–92.
11. The Greek terms designate a sleeping place and lying down to sleep.
12. Bernard Green, *Christianity in Ancient Rome: The First Three Centuries* (London: T&T Clark, 2010), 177.
13. Ibid.
14. Greg Laurie, *Twitter*, 6 April 2015 [cited 3 September 2015]. Available from the Internet: *https://twitter.com/greglaurie/status/585139658004135937*.

WEEK 3

1. C. S. Lewis, *The Screwtape Letters* (New York: HarperCollins, 1942), ix.
2. Jimmy Furr, "The Occult," *FAITH Discipleship: Faith Reaching Out to World Religions* (Nashville: LifeWay Press, 2001), 167–72.
3. Merrill F. Unger, *Biblical Demonology* (Grand Rapids, MI: Kregel, 1994), 62.
4. Peter Thomas O'Brien, *The Letter to the Ephesians, The Pillar New Testament Commentary* (Grand Rapids, MI: W. B. Eerdmans, 1999).
5. Avery T. Willis Jr., *MasterLife 3: The Disciple's Victory* (Nashville: LifeWay Press, 1996), 23–25.
6. William Gurnall, *The Christian in Complete Armor*, vol. 1 (Carlisle: Banner of Truth Trust, 2002), 87.

WEEK 4

1. Barna Group, *American Bible Society: State of the Bible 2015* (New York: American Bible Society/Barna Group, 2015).
2. Ibid.
3. Ibid.
4. Mark Twain, *goodreads* [cited 3 September 2015]. Available from the Internet: *www.goodreads.com*.
5. For a comprehensive assessment of the Islamic State, see Craig A. Evans and Jeremiah J. Johnston, *Jesus and the Jihadis* (Shippensburg: Destiny Image Publishing, 2015).
6. Professor Paul Maier, Christian Thinkers Society conference.
7. Harold Rawlings, *Trial by Fire* (Wellington: The Rawlings Foundation, 2004), 103.
8. Owen Jarus, "Mummy Mask May Reveal Oldest Known Gospel," *livescience* [online], 18 January 2015 [cited 3 September 2015]. Available from the Internet: *www.livescience.com/49489-oldest-known-gospel-mummy-mask.html*.
9. Professor Dan Wallace, presentations at Christian Thinkers Society events and in my Houston Baptist University classes on the remarkable way the early church movement formatted the Word of God.
10. Bart Ehrman, *Misquoting Jesus: The Story Behind Who Changed the Bible and Why* (San Francisco: HarperCollins, 2007), 90.
11. David S. Dockery, *The Doctrine of the Bible* (Nashville: Convention, 1991), 98–99.
12. Ibid., 100.
13. Ken Hemphill, *LifeAnswers: Making Sense of Your World* (Nashville: LifeWay, 1993), 39.
14. Scribal quote from GA Lect 402, A.D. 1079, presented by Dan Wallace to conclude his lecture "Formatting the Word of God," courtesy of the Center for the Study of New Testament Manuscripts.
15. Bruce Metzger at age 83, as quoted in Lee Strobel, *The Case for the Real Jesus* (Grand Rapids, MI: Zondervan, 2007), 99.
16. Ibid.

WEEK 5

1. "First WHO World Suicide Report," *World Health Organization* [online, cited 3 September 2015]. Available from the Internet: *www.who.int/mental_health/suicide-prevention/en/*.
2. Ibid.
3. "11 Facts About Suicide," *DoSomething.org* [online, cited 4 September 2015]. Available from the Internet: *www.dosomething.org/facts/11-facts-about-suicide*.
4. Justin Worland, "This Bill Could Help Veterans with Mental Health," *Time* [online], 6 February 2015 [cited 4 September 2015]. Available from the Intneret: *http://time.com/3694053/veteran-suicide/*.
5. "Suicide: Facts at a Glance" [online, cited 4 September 2015]. Available from the Internet: *www.cdc.gov/ViolencePrevention/pdf/Suicide_DataSheet-a.pdf*.
6. Sarah Eekhoff Zylstra, "1 in 4 Pastors Have Struggled with Mental Illness, Finds LifeWay and Focus on the Family," *Gleanings* [online], 22 September 2014 [cited 3 September 2015]. Available from the Internet: *www.christianitytoday.com/gleanings/2014/september/1-in-4-pastors-have-mental-illness-lifeway-focus-on-family.html*.
7. Ibid.
8. Stephen Altrogge, "Is Mental Illness Actually Biblical?"[cited 3 September 2015]. Available from the Internet: *www.biblestudytools.com/blogs/stephen-altrogge/is-mental-illness-actually-biblical.html*.
9. Marina Marcus, M. Taghi Yasamy, Mark van Ommeren, and Dan Chisholm, Shekhar Saxena, "Depression: A Global Public Health Concern" [online, cited 3 September 2015]. Available from the Internet: *www.who.int/mental_health/management/depression/who_paper_depression_wfmh_2012.pdf*.
10. Ronald C. Kessler, Katherine A. McGonagle, Shanyang Zhao, Christopher B. Nelson, Michael Hughes, Suzann Eshleman, Hans-Ulrich Wittchen, Kenneth S. Kendler, "Lifetime and 12-Month Prevalence of DSM-III-R Psychiatric Disorders in the United States: Results from the National Comorbidity Survey," *Arch Gen Psychiatry* 51, no. 1 (1994): 8–19.
11. Daniel Morehead, "Mental Health and the Church," *Leadership Network* [online, cited 3 September 2015]. Available from the Internet: *http://leadnet.org/mental-health-summit/*.
12. Cherese Jackson, "Another Pastor Commits Suicide," *Liberty Voice* [online], 19 April 2014 [cited 4 September 2015]. Available from the Internet: *www.guardianlv.com/2014/04/another-pastor-commits-suicide*.
13. "First WHO World Suicide Report."
14. Ibid.
15. "11 Facts About Suicide."
16. Justin Worland, "This Bill Could Help Veterans with Mental Health."
17. "Suicide: Facts at a Glance."
18. Arielle Eiser, "The Crisis on Campus," *American Psychological Association* [online], September 2011 [cited 4 September 2015]. Available from the Internet: *www.apa.org/monitor/2011/09/crisis-campus.aspx*.
19. Ibid.
20. Matthew Stucker, "Robin Williams' Death Ruled Suicide" *CNN* [online], 11 November 2014 [cited 4 September 2015]. Available from the Internet: *www.cnn.com/2014/11/07/showbiz/robin-williams-autopsy*.
21. Adapted from "Myths & Facts," *San Francisco Suicide Prevention* [online, cited 4 September 2015]. Available from the Internet: *www.sfsuicide.org/prevention-strategies/myths-and-facts/*.

WEEK 6

1. Walter Isaacson, *Steve Jobs* (New York: Simon & Schuster, 2011), 14.
2. C. S. Lewis, *Letters of C. S. Lewis* (Orlando: Harcourt Books, 1966), 477.
3. C. S. Lewis, *The Problem of Pain* (New York: Macmillan, 1962), 10.
4. Kevin Belmonte *D. L. Moody: A Life* (Chicago: Moody, 2014) 102.
5. Paul Copan, *That's Just Your Interpretation* (Grand Rapids, MI: Baker, 2001), 91.
6. Craig A. Evans and Jeremiah J. Johnston, *Jesus and the Jihadis: The Rage of ISIS* (Shippensburg, PA: Destiny Image, 2015).
7. I am indebted to my dear friend Professor Paul Copan for his participation with Christian Thinkers Society from the beginning but even more for his pastoral and philosophical training in helping me think through the experiential and intellectual issues of suffering and evil. Thank you for your faithfulness.
8. C. S. Lewis, *Mere Christianity* (New York: Macmillan, 1952), 45–46.
9. James MacDonald, *When Life Is Hard* (Nashville: LifeWay Press, 2010), 157.
10. Randy Alcorn, *If God Is Good* (Colorado Springs: Multnomah, 2010), 4.
11. Jeremiah J. Johnston, "Modern Day Martyrs: A Non-Christian's Chronicle of China's Dark Side," *Christian Research Journal* 35 (2012): 60.
12. Joel C. Gregory, *Growing Pains of the Soul* (Nashville: Thomas Nelson, 1987), 13.
13. MacDonald, *When Life Is Hard*, 133.

Did you love
UNANSWERED?
Maybe it's time to "like" it.

If your group enjoyed the *Unanswered Bible Study*, help us tell the world about it. Take a few moments to tweet, like, post, pin, and otherwise share the love in all your social media channels.

- Post a comment about this study at **facebook.com/groupsmatter**.

- Recommend *Unanswered* to your friends and other groups at your church.

- Here are a few tweets to consider:

  - "My questions are no longer **#Unanswered**. Check out the new Bible study from @JeremyJohnstonJ"

  - "Got questions? See how Christianity intersects with tough issues like suicide, ghosts, and more in **#Unanswered** from @JeremyJohnstonJ"

  - "My small group highly recommends new Bible study **#Unanswered** from @JeremyJohnstonJ"